D0112223

IN THE DESERT WE DO NOT COUNT THE DAYS

Stories & Illustrations
by John Brandi

HOLY COW! PRESS
DULUTH, MINNESOTA 1991

ISBN 0-930100-40-9 (paper)

Library of Congress Number: 90-82296

Essays or portions of stories in previous form have appeared in: *The New Mexico Humanities Review, The Denver Post, El Palacio, Coyote's Journal, River Styx, Longpond Review, Periodics, Towards the Twenty-first Century* (an anthology), *Courier* (a National Park Service newsletter), *The Spirit That Wants Me* (a New Mexico anthology), *Carlsbad Caverns Natural History Association Broadside Series*, and as *The Cowboy from Phantom Banks*, a book issued by Floating Islands Publications, 1982.

Special acknowledgment to the New Mexico Arts Division and the Nevada State Council on the Arts (funded by the National Endowment for the Arts) who awarded the author residencies during which the stories and drawings were completed for this book.

Author's Note: With respect to the privacy of the people whose lives are portrayed herein, some names have been changed. Resemblance of fictional characters to those of living persons is purely coincidental.

Publisher's Address:

Holy Cow! Press

P.O. Box 3170/Mt. Royal Station

Duluth, Minnesota 55803

Distributor's Address:

The Talman Company, Inc.

150 Fifth Avenue

New York, New York 10011

This project is supported, in part, by a grant from the National Endowment for the Arts in Washington, D.C., a Federal Agency.

TABLE OF CONTENTS

To my father, John Sr., for his keen eye.
To my brother Jim, whose off-road directions never fail to surprise.

It's the magic. How do ya teach 'em the magic?

THE COWBOY FROM PHANTOM BANKS

Old Jake Anderson, I'd give my life for him. He leased a whole township, thirty-six square miles I think it was, from the United States government. And that was barely enough to get by on considering it was mostly sand hills and dry flat.

Jake was such a relief from the ultra-conservative "squares" of the city. Squares like that dandruff-shouldered lady who eyeballed me up and down in the Salvation Army Thrift Store one day. I was lingering in the used book section. So was she. Finally she looked over and asked if I'd noticed any good history books on the rack. History and religion, that's what she was into. Nothing wrong with that, of course; it was just the way she was into it that soured my day.

"Yes," I told her, "there's one on the top shelf by John Gunther. *Inside Russia Today.*"

But the poor woman was put off, startled, eager to speak her word.

"Oh, I'm *very* sorry. I'm not interested in Communism. Only United States history."

She went about her business and I mine. But I felt that her eye was on me the whole time. And it was.

"Oh," she repeated. "Now here's a book I'll buy just to *burn*." A long silence followed. Obviously I was supposed to react. At length I fell for the bait. Coldly, though.

"Which one is it?"

She smiled, eyed my a-little-too-long hair, and drew a breath. "Oh, it's called *Communal Child Rearing in Contemporary USA*."

I had no comment. But she used the occasion to swiftly proceed into a monologue about how Rome fell because of its lack of morality, and how "we" were headed in the same direction. I eagerly made for the cash register with *The Complete Poems of Robert Frost*, and left. A real find. Twenty-five cents. Worth every bit of the encounter.

• • •

But, anyway, Jake Anderson. He was a cowboy. He'd played the rodeos. Trained horses, worked dude ranches, taught horsemanship, cattle-punched, wrote his own songs, played guitar, yodeled, and spilled out free-form and rhyming poems. He was an unexcelled storyteller. He drank Black Velvet whiskey and smoked like the dickens. He was in his mid-fifties and had a bright, young twenty-eight year old wife whom he called "sweetheart." They lived in a small trailer house, plunked down in the thornbrush next to a rusty windmill, a stocktank and a corral full of horses. No electricity, lots of snakes, red dust and Utah Phillips and Hank Williams on a battery-powered tape deck. You could float a horseshoe in Jake's cowboy coffee. You could grind the grounds between your teeth. He wasn't fooling with his songs, nor with his horses, nor with his lifestyle. Jake wasn't a closet cowboy nor a street corner cowboy. He didn't drink sissy coffee, and he didn't punch cows in a sissy way. He didn't drive a four-wheeler or fly a Piper Cub.

He'd get drunk. He'd hug me. It was man to man. Or it was woman to man. Kay, his wife, she'd track him down, chase him around the corral to give him his cancer treatment. Jake was dying. Patches of raw skin would be left on his arms and legs after her scraping, a process of keeping him alive which I never fully understood or accepted. The cowboy would scream. The pain would make him fantasize walking off into the milkweed, the mesquite, into the sand hills and rattlesnakes forever. People in town would tell him, "Jake quit your smoking. Jake c'mon into town and get a job." And Jake would silently retreat further into the life he'd always known. The horses, the cows, the dust, the guitar. Nothing romantic about it. His hands were like leather. His eyes like baked porcelain. His hat appeared to be nothing more than the very elements themselves, held together in electrical combinations not understood by the poet or layman.

Faded Hearts and Winter Roses, that's what he liked to sing. Or he'd talk about the saga of Frank and Clint at Oro Grande. He loved that one. And he loved to ride my case for always wanting to write down his stories and sayings. He was the cowpuncher version of Carlos Casteneda's Yaqui Don Juan of the Sonora Desert. But this was the Chihuahua. Called the "Trans-Pecos" by some. Less pretty than the Sonora, and far tougher, in my opinion. It wasn't a place you could safely come back to without a hat like Jake's or a guitar. But I had neither. Perhaps it was tomfoolery on my part, romantic.

I went there because I knew I could "get it." I was always immediately welcomed because, as Jake once admitted, he couldn't "get it" anywhere else. He was amused by the core of our relationship. The fact that he'd pegged me as a liberal, young, college-bred hipster. The fact that I thought he was a true redneck around the edges. So what? Humor the whole thing, that's what we did! He was so far right and I was so far left that our meeting hadn't anything to do with destiny. We were just two beings on the planet that happened to be full-circle right from the beginning.

"Christ, they got us down to 160 acres as it is. What's this environmental impact study? They comparin' this gol'blasted desert to some California truck farm, or what? We gonna let college students from back east get their trainin' by usin' us as guinea pigs or something? They wanna tell us, do this do that with coyotes or antelope. They zip, one two three, right through school on Rocky-feller grants then charge out here in faded jeans and notebooks, tellin' me to build my horse fence three feet high, or keep a hole in the sheep wire to let the endangered species through. They look at the broom-weed, tellin' me it's purdy, protect it.

"Now, you suppose they'd live here? How do you suppose anyone who's been sixteen years in school's gonna have an answer? You suppose they know the hamburger they'll grab on the road after they leave here's from a *cow*? God, if they took over we'd all starve. Goddamn, the environmentalist is runnin' the rancher out!"

Jake didn't trust schools. He claimed he'd quit public school in the eighth grade "to get an education." He also claimed to know more upside down and backwards than a kid fresh out of college. He was proud of that. His "koan" was simple. He'd put it to anyone fresh into the desert. It went like this (he wouldn't ask it, just speak it, and eyeball you to see if you understood):

"This is the only place I know where ya have to dig for wood and climb for water."

I remember once, we were talking about my attempts to get high schoolers to express themselves through music and poetry. Jake drew a long toke on his Vantage cigarette ("Can't smoke this brand—it's like runnin' against the wind with my mouth open") and said:

"John, I dunno if ya can work with teenagers. I think they've done gone, done escaped. I'd teach 'em how to live, not just how to exist. If you really wanta give 'em somethin' to think about ya oughta order fifty fiddlers like ol' Hiram Posie from Crow Flat . . .

"That's sacred music—

"And as for po-ems, well, I figgure ya gotta make one of them six-five marijuana-smokin' basketball players come outta one of your poetry classes high on just the word, ya know? He's gotta look down at his little sweetheart and slip his arm around her, sayin'—'Honey, I just wrote me a po-em!'"

He was right. He knew about music. About the muse. The origins and the power of the word. About the importance of living on the edge. He'd emphasize it over and over again: "Teach 'em to live, teach 'em to *live*! It's not the money. There's a difference between makin' it financially and livin'. If ya live, then life pretty well takes care of itself. Whadda ya learn in school, huh? How to legitimately rob banks through business, or how to cheat on income taxes? Tell me, do they teach magic? They got a way of measurin' magic? They got any programs that get you *out* there, get you a little *hungry* for once? Poverty, nakedness, hunger. Those are things make a man learn *fast*. Why, these kids ain't gone hungry unless they didn't get home from huntin' on time for lunch!"

I'm condensing this for the sake of the reader, of course. It never came quite so fast and heavy. But it came. Here and there, mending fence wires, driving an hour or so through the sand hills, across the Pecos into town for supplies, going up to have a look at the pump, and so on. Coffee, steaks, sand and cows. It was a neighborly sort of thing. Near neighbors in that country, hell—they could be a hundred miles apart. A star was nearer. Or the damn mysterious "lights" that swept over the desert in the purple night.

"The kind of lights no one sees 'cause they're all inside watchin' TV, and TV, aw—John! It's what keeps people from tellin' stories anymore. I think I know my neighbors a hundred miles away better than some folks in town who sit right in the same room front of that TV with their next-door neighbors."

Once I persuaded Jake to visit one of my classes to tell stories. Right at the climax, the punch line of his saga of Frank and Clint at Oro Grande, the bell rang. The students hurried away. None stayed to thank him for his tales; nor even for the fifty-mile drive over the bumps and ruts out of the sand country to the south of town. Jake couldn't be convinced to return after that. In his bitter moments he'd size the whole thing up:

"Days of teachin' is over. All you're doin' is baby-sittin'. You help 'em get a diploma, but what's education without experience? Those BLM people, for example, the ones that came out here—hell, they couldn't even lay a pipe from here to there in a straight line. Not without transit and machinery. Christ, any cowboy could lay a pipe— we used to level three hundred feet at a time by usin' a length of hose filled with water, 'cause when water came out both ends, we knew things was level.

"So I see it this way. Parents, teachers—what some of 'em do best these days is to protect their kids to the point of robbin' them of any individuality. Nothin's tied together for kids anymore. I mean—they can't tie it together in their own heads. School's there, life's here, cowboy's in the movies, lunch comes from the counter, bread's wrapped in a sack at the store. Water comes from the pipe. Like that. Like *that*?

"Aw, John. It's the magic. The magic's missin'! How do ya teach 'em the magic?"

Jake's south of Loving, on a fifty-mile left out of Malaga, some-where between Phantom Banks and Rustler Bluff. And, yes—those are real names. You should look him up if you can. He comes into town once and awhile. You'll recognize him by the hat and the hands.

Ain't nowhere y' can't go if y' don't get tied down t' what y' think y' own.

ZEN AND THE
ART OF TRUCKING

We can get the hay loaded by nightfall and he'll be ready to go. It's 427 miles—through Eunice, Tarzan, Sweetwater and Abilene—to Fort Worth. W.D. can master the trip nonstop, with ten gears forward and 300 gallons of fuel to the last drop. But the drive, a couple times per week, plus loading and unloading the hay, plus occasional breakdowns (the last one in Muleshoe), plus trying to maintain a family back in Carlsbad—can give a man his share.

Last time we were filling the tanks of W.D.'s red and white Peterbilt, he was bidding good-by for a week, and I was complaining about a wart on my left index finger and how the hay needles had gotten into it. "Give it a couple drops of battery acid on a matchstick," he told me. If that don't work, keep the wart soaked with castor oil 'til it falls off." Finally, he recommended old Mrs. Cisneros, in Loving, whose specialty was delivering babies and curing warts. "Careful, though," he laughingly warned, "she might use cat innards or fried garlic."

It was getting dark. To the east a big yellow moon rose over the high desert plain. In places an ignited flame of natural gas burned from an escape above a well. There was no archetypal coyote yodel or anything "western" like jangling spurs or horse-clop or buckboard squeak. Instead, there was a background of diesel locomotives on the Southern Pacific tracks and tank trucks thundering down the line toward Pecos, Texas. In W.D.'s haylot, there was the strong stench of refined oil, liquefied sunlight. Of axle grease, cow dung and human sweat. And of baled alfalfa—forty tons of it, fermenting on the rear trailer of his cab-over Peterbilt.

I was wiping the windows, he was pumping diesel fuel into the twin tanks from his private pump under a tin shed. We were looking out into the approaching dusk, our talk gradually following a line of rhythm from the weather to the plains to the Fort Worth highway to the Goodnight-Loving Trail to lightning and Indians and nomads. Then we got on this thing about endangered species. I was talking about the desert pupfish, certain species of pincushion cactus and the countless times I'd seen fat human beings crunch vinegarroons or praying mantis under their leather-soled feet. W.D., however, had another point of view:

"Y'ask me, the real endangered sorts is what we got so few of nowadays. The individual. I mean someone who decides things for himself. A free thinker."

At that instant, like many times before, I caught W.D. inside my eyes as a kind of big-hatted, trucker-philosopher. As gentleman, welder, jack-of-all-trades, haylot manager, construction worker, self-taught engineer and family man. As he went around banging on the tires with a steel rod, I seemed to hear the voice of an ancient Zen Master:

"If y'don't get it from yourself, where will you go for it?"

I was always cautious when acknowledging his statements of wisdom. I feared anything other than a casual nod would offend his easy style. I remember once he was standing on the O-most-holy-and-symbolic Peterbilt door ladder, saying something like:

"Ain't nowhere y'can't go if y'don't get tied down t'what y'think y'own."

He was mumbling all sorts of things about not letting your property "own" you or your car "own" you or your church "own" you or even your daydreams "own" you.

"Some of us even let our *differences* own us," he twinkled.

W.D. was born and raised on the south end of town. He was a radical in disguise, and yet he didn't seem to be too disturbed by driving north on Canal Street into the heart of his desert hometown: a neat little Republican spread with a Fundamentalist church on every other corner, trim motels, squat two-bedroom Eisenhower-era homes with bomb shelters out back and ladies in beehive hairdos and kids acting smart in their raised-up 4-wheel drives. W.D. was more tolerant of that society than I could ever be. He'd be patient with the talk of a liberal or a conservative, weed out what was valuable for him as an individual, and go on with things. But I'd bite my nails. I'd go crazy when a street-preacher would interrupt my routine in front of the drug store or post office, whereas W.D. would immediately size-up the preacher and gradually nurse him away from the gospel and into his past lives as a biplane stunt man or crop duster. Me, I'd be stuck with my prejudice against look-alike homes and what kind of people I assumed lived in them. W.D., he could walk right into a stucco pre-fab neighborhood and sniff out a retired circus clown and coax him to talk about his days under the big top as a "human pretzel." Or he'd discover a woman faith-healer, a bus-driver poet from the depression days, or a near-blind polar explorer who'd hung around with Admiral Byrd.

When I got to loading hay with W.D. we'd always talk about these

13

things. Or we'd talk about trucks or the price of baled horse feed or barrels of gasoline. Or about the highway. "Y'gotta drive with one eye on the road, another couple to either side, and one on the hay for spare measure. Y'go down the road with all of 'em workin' at once, yet seein' things in order—as if they was just one." And then darkness would fall and it'd be time for dinner or time to haul off toward the Texas line, the big yellow blinkers flashing and the gears beginning to grind.

W.D. didn't like the word "religion" much, which is the sign of a true religious person. He wouldn't have heard a word of it if I were to say this to his face, but I always saw the man as a kind of Good Shepherd whose faith was in the *living* of life, doing the ordinary things "right." From there on it was "barefootin' it all the way," as truckers say.

"If y'know your wheels, y'don't need no chains to keep traction."

La musica! The desert breathes with confetti and strumming guitars. The fossil hills applaud with distant echoes, crowned by trumpeting rays of sun.

CONFESSIONS OF A NEIGHBORHOOD SPY

A cross the street are five cars parked in the driveway of a neat
plankboard house with a bright blue tar-shingle roof. The family
who lives there is transplanted from Mexico and surrounded by
neighbors who are, for the most, dyed-in-the-wool church-going
whites. On Sundays Mrs. Smith—who once despairingly eyed me and
said "the desert is dead"—watches the Mexican family as she pretends
to search for fallen pecans in her front yard. She's waiting for her
Catholic neighbors to go to church. Their church, her church, any
church. It doesn't really matter. Just so they set the day aside for
Divine Providence.

On Wednesdays it's Mrs. Anderson's turn to keep track of the
"aliens," as she calls them—even though they've lived in the neighborhood for seven years now. She's ready to sic the First Free Will Full
Gospel Baptist Church bus on them—one of a number of goodwill
buses that come around with free pillowcases and linen and canned

hominy and lima beans and plenty of religious pamphlets and an itinerant preacher who won't quit once he gets started. Mrs. Anderson really prefers that the Mexican Family attend her church, not Mrs. Smith's.

Then there is Mrs. Harris—whose teenage son was recently struck by lightning along with five other boys while piling themselves into a human pyramid at the Philmont Scout Ranch. Mrs. Harris' favorite pastime is to peer from her living room curtains, one eye on her soap opera, the other on guard, waiting for the Mexican family's toy collie to nose around her aluminum garbage cans and lift its leg to pee—so she can ring the animal control officer (known as a dogcatcher in most communities). She seems to have a fondness for doing this. For watching the Sanchez family's kids scream and plead when the blue-uniformed officer arrives with his little black can of mace and his steel clipboard with yellow citation notices ready to be written.

And then there is me, right along with everyone else, keeping tabs on the entire scenario. "Life history class," would be my reply if anyone were to ask what I'm doing staring from my upper-story flat between the bougainvilleas and the typewriter. What I have primarily observed is that the household across the street, despite this conservative neighborhood's push for it to conform to an American way of life, maintains its own ritual.

On Sundays, three men arrive with their musical instruments in three separate automobiles. They prefer to speak their native Spanish, and carry their accessories in pink-and-yellow-checkered nylon bags with plastic handles: a can of pop, a couple of Tecates, a dozen homemade tortillas wrapped in cloth, a light sweater or jacket for the cooling twilight hours. The first to arrive is usually Andres, driving a rust-pocked powder-blue Valiant with one headlight. He rolls Velvet tobacco into thin smokes and puffs for a long time in his front seat before he walks to the Sanchez's door. The second man to arrive is Esequiel, weaving up in a vintage forest-green '51 Chevrolet pickup with plastic buckets of pig slop in the bed. He brakes, puts a rock under the rear wheel, then lifts out his ancient guitar with which he will complement Andres' Honer accordion. The third man comes along by foot, harmonica in his sport-coat pocket, wearing a pair of taped-together dark glasses over his albino face. He is named Alba, Spanish for "dawn."

Sometimes—like today, the Mexican feast called Day of the Dead—they sit on the front porch with one big extended family of friends and relatives gathered round, tuning voices and instruments for a Sunday of song. A basket of sweet rolls. A little beer and coffee. The perpetual sodas, of course. And lime-spiced bowls of *menudo*. In most south-of-the-border neighborhoods there would soon be colorful clusters of men, women and children coming out from all corners to hear these song makers. But here, no. The widows behind their shades remain aloof, given over to moral and rational criticism inside their swamp-coolered living rooms.

> *"Tomasa,Tomasa . . .*
> *She greets you with a big warm hug.*
> *Tomasa, Tomasa . . .*
> *She invites you in for tamales*
> *while her husband's at the pub."*

And so passes the Day of the Dead—much to Mrs. Smith's dismay, to Mrs. Anderson's distaste, to Mrs. Harris' repressed desire. The vermilion ball of sun lingers over the horseshoe-shaped uplift of fossil hills to the west—the remains of a barrier reef formed around an inland sea 250,000,000 years ago. The desert floor upon which we sit is filled with makeshift accordion music, a sweet but badly-tuned guitar, and the cupped, warbling notes of Alba's harmonica. A skyrocket whinnies through the mother-of-pearl air. A young child is asleep beneath an embroidered blanket on the grass. Others climb through the silver hexagrams of a monkey-bar set. Overhead, pumpkin-colored cumuli billow and fuzz out at the edges, hanging with cross-stitches of rain that tantalize the earth but never touch down.

And—*la musica!* Nothing about it is meant to be perfect. It is meant only for enchantment; that the afternoon and all the people in it be transformed with joy and camaraderie; be in a mood other than the despairing one they might have been in before the three whiskered bards took to their strings and keys and soundboxes. Union of voices, union of spirit. Union of sounds, union of bodies. A magical twilight. A dream, slowly freeing itself from reality. My windows are open wide. The bougainvilleas lift their flaming heads in applause. The pomegranate tree in the front yard is shaking its leaves.

During the rest of the week it is work and school for the family across the street. Mr. Sanchez rises before dawn and waters the lawn, even if it is mid January and below freezing. Even if the grass has long withered and gone into its winter sleep. I often imagine him watering flowers in the eternal warmth of the tropical zone of Veracruz; and wonder about our inappropriate term "temperate zone" for the northern latitudes, where the sun drops low in winter and all but the hardiest plants wither.

After his watering routine, when the morning light finally starts to break, Mr. Sanchez takes a dry rag and wipes all the windows of the station wagon. He does the same to the Cougar, the Pinto, the Monte Carlo, and the half-running Trans-Am. Now come the kids, outside to watch their father move the cars around so he can back the Cougar out of the driveway for Mrs. Sanchez. Sonia, Leticia, Francis, Geraldo, Lidia, Marco, Angela and Chico—they are there on the porch or round about in the yard receiving the first tangerine rays of desert sun, their breath vaporized into delicate curlicues as they converse. Finally Señora Sanchez appears from the front door. She is dressed immaculately in hospital white, a black net over her permed hair, a pair of soft-soled plastic shoes on her feet. She waves good-by to her children and leaves each of them a set of instructions for the day, then strolls through the carbon-monoxide haze of the idling Cougar. With a rattling of ill-timed pistons, she is off.

It is Mr. Sanchez's turn now—in the Pinto. A black lunchpail, a thermos of cinnamon-spiced coffee, sap-stained work clothes, a green nylon baseball cap. He'll drive the three miles to Lolo Vigil's where he's been employed for three years, and spend the day as he has every day in Lolo's timber yard: peeling bark from young fir trunks to be used as *vigas*—ceiling beams; and skinning juniper branches to serve as *latillas* to be placed across the *vigas* in herringbone ceiling patterns. Architectural elements indigenous to this part of the Southwest.

It is a diligent and honorable kind of labor. Lolo himself, now in his eighties, is a virtuous hard-working man who upholds a long tradition of minimal machinery, maximum handiwork. He stresses quality over quantity, never giving in to trend, never swooned by numbers or demand. He supplies not only building materials like those described, but hires Mr. Sanchez and men like him to weave willows into garden and greenhouse trellises; to build pine-wood doors; to carve corbels, lintels; even panels for confessional boxes in churches. They make coffins as well, and cribs for newborns— gracefully bending and nailing river willows into original basket and boat-like shapes. Yet, for all their skill and original know-how, Mr. Sanchez and his kind are known by most Americans as "unskilled laborers"—immigrants from another country who work for minimum wage and don't make demands on their employer.

Back home, the younger kids trail off to school—oblivious to time. Like me, when I was small, they sometimes don't make it. They get distracted in the cotton fields or dandelion meadows. They sidetrack into the pollywog ponds where the pavement dead ends. They find their way to Jolly Thomas' horse corrals where clowns practice with bulls; where dappled ponies are bred for circus shows.

Leticia—the oldest daughter—has remained home for over a month now, her hand bandaged since the day she lost a finger in the bread-slicing machine at Cora's Bakery. In her thin black nightrobe, her eyes accented with ice green and her cheeks painted heliotrope, she is a teenage panther whose padded feet make no sound when she walks. She looks in the mirror, waters the geranium plants inside the window, herds the collie back into the laundry room when the animal control officer arrives. When he drives off, after a short visit with Mrs. Harris across the street, Leticia heaves Chico's football at the exhaust trail of the dogcatcher's truck, cusses, and releases her toy collie from the laundry room. The dog yips and trots straight for Mrs. Harris' garbage cans again. And the replay begins. With everybody in the neighborhood carefully hiding behind half-closed curtains pretending to be keeping to themselves.

It doesn't seem that anyone in the Sanchez family is *that* odd. It's the people behind their curtains that strike me as peculiar. It isn't strange to me to see Mrs. Sanchez arriving in the desert twilight driving slowly down East Rose with her headlights off, flicking them on only at important intersections, to save the battery. Or turning the ignition off—to save gas—coasting most of the last lap to her driveway. Nor is it strange to see Mr. Sanchez take his dry rag to each and every automobile window to begin the day—surely a procedure more important to the machine's health than a good tune-up or timing check! I've watched this whole episode on the other side of the line. I've seen the same archetypal mother meticulously sweep her earthen patio after sprinkling it with water (which is Saturday's rite across the street, only the reed broom has been replaced by a nylon one). I've seen a thousand jaguar-like Leticias in heliotrope makeup stirring coffee in the mirror. I've watched fathers and mothers, children and relatives, friends and neighborhoods gather round a trio of musicians like Andres, Ezequil and Alba. I've heard rockets fizz and Tecate cans pop on the Day of the Dead. Watched lovers exchange sugar skulls, and brass bands play for the deceased in cemeteries decorated with crepe.

On which side of the street do these neighbors who pretend to exemplify "America the Free" stand? They peer, unhappy and alone, behind drawn blinds. It is Sunday and all of outdoors is one big church! Listen, while life-giving cries erupt from kids running out from under their tar-shingled roof. Watch, as they tack fiery pin-wheels to lilac trees to celebrate the return of ancestral presences. Music opens the door to the dream. The desert *isn't* dead. It breathes with confetti and strumming guitars. The fossil hills applaud with distant echoes, crowned by trumpeting rays of sun. Brachiopods, algae, ancient corals all begin to sing:

Viva la musica!

Everyone is united inside the metaphor between this world and the next. It is Sunday, Day of the Dead. Through the window my spirit flies. I join a garden party in the center of Eden. And toast a foamy Tecate to celebrate the intoxication of this, worthy-of-being-lived-to-its-fullest, life!

The little barn has just enough segments of siding missing to create an inside effect similar to the lighting of Le Corbusier's famous chapel in France.

A VISIT TO JULIAN'S
BLACKSMITH SHOP

I cough and look at the three-quarter moon, a wet towel around my neck. It is impossible to make love. Downstairs, the Texan rough-neck and his wife have been up most of the night arguing about their last argument. Upstairs, the eaves rattle, the desert wind charges through the ceiling like a hot river, a crimson stag in heat. Dust fills the cerebrum and sags in the testicles. The lady of my dreams twists and turns; the sheets are wet. Finally she wakes saying she's been swimming in a huge, white-billowed wave, something out of a delicately-colored Hokusai print. But I am firmly planted in tongue-parched New Mexico, unable to catch a wink. The fine, gray Chihua-hua sand filters in the window cracks and covers every map on our wall. The steel bannister beyond our outside door, even in the middle of night, is too hot for the hand. Worse, there is an exploding gas well east of town gasping with a hundred feet of flame, snorting a putrid stench into the atmosphere from deep within the desert's bowels—

12,000 feet down. The wind funnels the fiery lashing up from the 200-million year-old Permian limestone and carries it this way, brings the bitter taste of melted steel from Brahaney's drilling rig, collapsed above the well.

At dawn there is soot on the horizon, and a distant pall of tan smoke from the potash mines—but the wind has died. There must be a hundred tumbleweeds piled between the wrecked Rambler and rusted pickup-truck shells turned upside down behind the apartment. Beyond lie the December cotton fields with torn stalks and exploded fibers caught in the barbed wire at the edge of the farmsteads. And then, far beyond, there is a smudge of machinery: the U.S. Government Waste Isolation project—that foolhardy hole designed to "permanently" store low-level plutonium-contaminated garbage. All the radioactive waste that the Department of Energy has failed to manage from fifty years of nuclear bomb production and power plant operation.

Goats nag at the dripless water spigot two stories down—or is it one? My eyes are too blurry to see. They are as red as the gas flames that continue to pour from the plains toward the tiny village of Loving. I've gone through all the early hours sleepless. It wasn't too long ago that one could walk into the desert out there and come to know silence, come to discover a sort of infant self in solitude, to regain a sense of instinct. Now the land is filled with junk. It's been drilled into, blasted away, mined, overturned and criss-crossed with potholed roads. Rabbits don't go near the old water sources. They are no longer fit for drinking.

·   ·   ·

Today, Monday, I visit the local blacksmith and we talk about the wind and the fire. Julian's mainly concerned with his blacksmith's shed, which has been standing—radically leaning east or west according to the desert winds—for 47 years. "Oh, it goes this way 'n that, but I ain't scared. I'll get Bob to come over with his tractor 'n put the blade against the place to sit 'er up straight again."

The eighty year old man adjusts his cap and goes to work at the forge, heating worn and broken plowshares and hammering them back into shape on his anvil. In the short time I'm with him, a farmer arrives needing a custom-made wood-splitting wedge; a rancher orders two branding irons; someone else wants a feed trough; a woman brings in a design for a fireplace grille. They all talk about the wind, and ask Julian about his shop.

"Been here this long makin' whatever needs t'be made. Reckon another blow won't hurt this place none."

It's true that the place itself is a miracle. The little barn has just enough segments of siding missing to create an inside effect similar to the lighting of Le Corbusier's famous chapel in France. And the missing planks serve to let the wind through, rather than have it drive against the sides and blow the whole shed down.

"Suppose y'know there's a trailer home blowed over a quarter mile down the road? Wind tore it over last night and this mornin' they ripped it in half trying' t'place it rightside up again. But my little place, it's solid as ever. I come out here last night and put a couple props t'the east side. But I knew she'd hold. We always make it."

Besides his expertise as a blacksmith, Julian's an avid landscape painter. Weekends find him packed and ready to explore another sandy arroyo leading into the cool slopes of the Guadalupe Mountains. Or up on a high cliff, his easel tied to an alligator juniper, overlooking a rocky crevice filled with bigtooth maples and redbark madrone. On one of these excursions I accompanied him as an apprentice painter. We threw our gear—two easels and a box of paints, turps, brushes and canvases—into the bed of my pickup and drove upstream along a brook percolating clear as soda water over shelves of limestone; a stream that eventually soaked into the desert and never quite made it to the Pecos River.

When the road gave out we packed up our things and hiked into the sponge-like formations of a chalky canyon, refreshed by a breeze, overwhelmed by vertical walls etched with Permian marine fauna and spiral nautiloids.

I clearly remember Julian halting, looking up from the shadow of his floppy canvas hat, and remarking, "It's mystery enough just t'be alive. What can y'see with your imagination that's more astounding than right here where we're walking?"

That was the day the breeze turned into a full-fledged dust storm before noon. But our easels were firmly tied down with ropes and tent stakes and Julian insisted we keep on working—despite the sand sticking to our paintings. "It's okay, okay. Jus' leave her there, let the sand be part of the work, let it dry into the paint. That's what we're out here for—t'capture it."

I didn't argue. It was enjoyable to think of the grit and dust blowing into our paintings as part of a cosmic plan. I thought of Van Gogh with candles in his hat, sketching his Starry Night. Or Monet, his beard full of cadmium yellow, his head baked, trudging home across cliffs and rocks after a strenuous day in the field, not lightly equipped.

Driving out onto the hardpan of the desert again, a sea of peach-colored clouds above us at dusk, I asked Julian about that hole that government officials have told the locals is necessary to isolate radioactive toxins for at least 10,000 years. I can't quite describe the look on his face when I brought that subject up. He seemed amused but he wasn't smiling. He kind of bent his head down low then raised it up again, and all I could distinguish from the corner of my right eye was a whiskered silhouette in the passenger seat, gazing longingly into the swallow-darting dusk.

"Guess it'll give the depressed miners some work for awhile. But what human, tell me, can look into a crystal ball and say what th' future'll be like 150 lifetimes from now? We could have another flood, y'know. The sand could become a sea again. All that pluton stuff could float right up to the surface real easy. It just ain't outta sight because it's going into a hole.

"Looks t'me like man's still tryin' t'change places with God, some. He thinks he can see a hundred centuries into the future. He's got a tie on and a clipboard and he comes to these community meetings and he's gonna tell me that this radioactive stuff's just fine sealed off under the earth. He's gonna tell me things don't change in 10,000 years. He's gonna hold up a little paper suit and say, 'Just slip it on if the stuff leaks or spills and you'll be protected.' Well, ain't none of us out here crazy enough t'be *that* sure!"

• • •

After my visit to Julian's blacksmith shop I walk home through the cotton fields, feeling a great reverence for this man who still earns his living as he did nearly fifty years ago when he first came to Otis. I've got a sympathetic feeling for the family whose trailer-home blew over, too—and Brahaney Drilling, whose well blew out Thursday. But somehow that feeling doesn't touch me in quite the same place as the one I have for Julian. What moves me is the image of a man, soft-spoken and wise, in touch with himself through his craft, high-hearted and holding on—despite the technology that's rapidly cutting in on him.

There's probably a lot more to say, but it'll have to wait for another time. I'm carrying that forge smell now, and I feel good. I see the old man's hand on the hammer with sparks dancing through the dark barn. His eyebrows jump with the syncopated blows of metal. His bandana flaps in his rear pocket. Julian's face is determined, clear.

Why, it wasn't that long ago I remember him stepping away from his easel, then coming over to answer my request for a little advice, and looking up, down, around; even ducking his head under his legs to observe the world upside down. He laughed loudly, eyed me like a prankster, olew his nose into his red handkerchief, then gestured toward my easel and back again to the canyonscape.

"If you wanna learn t'paint, jus' paint, that's all. And don't be afraid of mistakes. Your only mistake is not trying. You've gotta glean from everywhere. You can't be closed to any of it. Even what you mistake for a barrier will wink back at you if you jus' give it th' eye."

I hope I'll have that look in my eye at eighty. And live in a place that knows how to ride with a storm, rather than be pushed down.

On the horizon one dust devil rises inside another . . .

OVER, INTO MEXICO

A visionary town, worn thin on the horizon. Flattened, baked—scoured by wind and seared by lightning. Briar hedges here, skeletal buildings there. Adobe facades that resemble geodes—thick and round, with dark crystal doorways, empty and ancient. In the corners of the sky's giant red eye, dust has collected. On the ground, hardly anyone is around. Just a couple of young men beneath an old Ford flatbed fixing a transmission. And a girl with her brother, wearing backwards baseball caps, unloading a BB gun. Under the desert sun, the streets are warped. They look as if any minute they might lift off and bend like wings, carrying the whole village into the Great Void. Facing the deserted plaza is a yellowed *tienda* with a fluorescent red flag flapping against a sagging doorway, advertising meat. From the belfry of the old mission, the Angelus rings. But there is no bell, no rope, no acolyte. And I am afraid to mention the word "ghost."

In the cemetery, bronze crucifixes gleam from fresh scrubbings of lemon and soda given to them on the Day of the Dead. I can imagine all sorts of smiling, weeping families appearing from the deep gullies of surrounding mountains, walking miles out of cracks and fissures with precious buckets of limply-splashing water, with mops and sponges, gathering over the graves of their loved ones to clean the headrests, to replace faded plastic roses with new ones. But there are no footprints, no orange peels, not the slightest remnant to show that someone was here. Not even my own feet leave a mark, nor does a shadow trail my body in the luminous sun. Perhaps I am not here; I am being imagined by someone else; cast upon this oppressive blankness by a body beyond this self that moves and feels and thinks and listens to a separate heartbeat.

On the horizon one dust devil rises inside another. At the perimeters of the graveyard a ghetto of weeds eats away at the dust-drifted footpath that circumambulates the headstones. Within a few weeks of the ceremonial cleaning, a congregation of hairy tumbleweeds has piled up against the barbed-wire fence enclosing the cemetery. The fresh plastic roses have once again faded. The elaborate wreathes, shaped like swans and castles and hearts, have withered into scattered fiber. So much for our lives—they are like paths opened from storms, bodies born from flowers, parched valentines slowly withering in the wind.

It is impossible to detect a hint of glory here. The town has risen its forehead just enough out of the earth to take a peek at civilization, then blink once or twice and return mute and dumb, back into its body. And the wind, it moves over the exposed plain like an all-knowing, all-cleansing, translucent serpent. It purifies the air with an oceanic taste, a salty tantalizing sting carried from afar. In it stand two skinny mares, their faces blank, their tails whipping from their rumps like black flames. Behind the mares, out of nowhere, a ragged man appears whose left shoulder is looped with bailing wire. He disappears towards the cemetery, probably going to tie down his uncle's grave in the wind.

For a moment, I wonder whether to ask for directions. But to where, and where in God's name have I come from? My ears thirst for a song, a laugh, a cock crow, the creak of a wagon wheel, the deep rattle of a raven, the redolent buzz of a hummingbird. But my ears go on thirsting. All is inaudible, lost to silence. I am in this place only as a memory; every footstep I take is a memory. And that is what I cannot quite comprehend—that the present tense has evaporated, cracked, fallen back on me as dust, as shards, as weightless ash with not enough substance or body to be examined. There's only space—vast, ominous, without melody—tempting me to fill it with words, with whatever I want to make of it, with whatever I want to believe true.

Enough . . .

Fine sand is filtering up my sleeves and down my collar. Any rut that leads roughly southwest toward Chihuahua City will do. This is a dehydrated and godforsaken place which beckons no one to stay. Perhaps it was abandoned because it suddenly found itself in the 20th century, smack in the middle of a Mexican Air Force artillery range. Who can know? But I think I'd rather let its mystery overpower the imagination—for this site, called only "El Hueso" on the maps, is just barely hanging on. The desert is king here—and about to eat it through.

His legs end in stubs. Likewise his arms. The paintbrush is held between two rounded stumps of bone and skin.

THE MAN BEHIND IXTACCÍHUATL ON A SUNDAY MORNING

Old Juarez, with leaf shadows covering the park sidewalks and Tarahumaras selling pecans under gargoyles. Tired mothers dressed in dark attire stroll past phone poles tacked with bulls and masked wrestlers. Record shops open early and compete with cathedral bells. At the central market there are tangerines in open bins, blood on the concrete floor, white calla lilies in crystal vases over meat-colored melons. A goat's head bakes over yellow coals, on a brazier above a table of ceramic demons who spit flowers from their erotic mouths. In a corridor smelling of bananas and fresh coffee, a trio of ragged musicians gets ready for a song. A blind man lifts his cane and lets it drop to the sidewalk through his fingers, lets it bounce up again into his hands, keeping staccato rhythm to the melody makers.

On Insurgentes, a young woman adjusts her false eyelashes and smooths her pants leg, straightens her bra and moves on. A vendor peddles velvet portraits of Che Guevara and Elvis Presley. The streets are mobbed. But the crowd is quiet in its apparent chaos. There is direction, purpose, grace here. Those who are not moving are stopped in perfect calmness. In this town, the total release from having anything "to do" is an honorable occupation of its own. Loitering is raised to a high art. Men open their collars and scan the morning headlines. Boys kick soccer balls under the trees. Women in flowery neons blend into hedges. They buy pineapples for their children, and stop to look over rows of pink plastic batmen. At one end of the park a Sunday painter has his easel propped in spotted shadows. He is immaculately dressed in a white shirt and pressed trousers. A tin cup to one side of his canvas hangs below a hand-lettered sign that says: "*Ayudame.*"

I join a small gathering around the painter, feeling a certain magnetism as the man raises and lowers his brush toward a half-painted volcano. His body is lit from within. His shirt is stuffed with light. His paintbrush creates counter-shadows in the bolting rays of morning sun. Now that I'm closer, I realize just how extraordinary his landscape of Ixtaccíhuatl is. And how amazing that he's dressed himself so flawlessly and with such precision. For the man has no hands or feet. His legs end in stubs. Likewise, his arms. The paintbrush is held between two rounded stumps of bone and skin. Yet he moves accurately, without hesitation. The man is copying Ixtaccíhuatl from a picture postcard held to the bottom of his easel by two rubber bands.

I linger nearly an hour with the painter. Doves flap around him as he lifts his brush. An organ's soft, nasal melody carries over from the cathedral. The man is composed like a god, a serious child at work, a monk illuminating a holy manuscript, a young girl at her very first mirror. Only once, during the time I am beside him, does the man break his powerful concentration and look away from his work. It is when a sudden darkness overcomes the park.

A drunk has floundered through the bushes. He's ready for a

brawl, breaks up a soccer game, spins his coat wildly over his head, snapping his sleeves this way and that. Traffic stops, the grackles take cover in the trees. With a firm stare in the direction of the vagabond, the painter sets down his brush. A shadow moves over the crest of Ixtaccíhautl. As if a secret code has been issued, the people in the park collectively respond to the spinning gaze of the artist. They begin to hiss and boo, louder and louder, until the drunk cannot stand the sudden change of energy. Bewildered, he retreats from the park, kicks his foot in a fury, does a Charlie Chaplin walk with a loose heel on his right shoe. A breeze nips him from behind, sending up miniature cyclones of gum wrappers.

The man behind Ixtaccíhuatl wets his brush with cadmium yellow and returns to illuminate the sky around his mountain. The park falls back into its quiet order. Traffic moves. Blackbirds descend from their high perches. Taxi men rhythmically splash water from tin cans over their dusty hubcaps. The cathedral bells win out over the blaring record parlors.

I cannot help being touched by the incident—the collective effort to reduce the drunk man's anger and gracefully put him away. It is as if nothing at all has happened to disturb the morning peace. I move closer to the painter and place two coins in his cup, knowing it to be a small offering. Again, I notice his stubs, his intense concentration. I feel the easy glow of light splintering in all directions, a corona from around his straw hat and body in the spotted shadows in the old park over the Sunday sidewalks of Juarez.

Innocent birth of furor. Immense opening of the terribly visible and transfixed.

ECSTASY AT
CONCHOS GORGE

W hen you pronounce "Conchos Gorge" with a heavy gringo
accent, it becomes "Conscious Gorge." Highway 16 bumps
through the desert across the Mexican border and takes you there. A
small warning in red letters on the road map reads:

INQUIRE LOCALLY WHEN LEAVING
MAIN HWY FOR DIRT ROADS

Gradually, the route zigzags up a solid rock outcrop and gives way
to a tremendous chasm of black light. From hundreds of feet below
comes an uprush of air bringing sweet and cold smells: narrowleaf
willow, swallow dung, delicate scents of pennyroyal, sharp wafts of
river-soaked moss, an occasional nose-wallop of decomposing bones.
The gorge speaks with a hollow, steady breathing. The water cuts
along swiftly, no time to clear its throat or give a yawn. The "Conscious River," as I like to rename it, scintillates with luminous
carnelions and deep ambers at the bottom of the lunatic crevasse it

has formed. Overhead, the sun's incandescent lamp flares its corona and keeps a steady pace across the sunburnt plateau.

I pull the emergency brake on my truck and place a rock under the rear wheel. Looking south, there's an unending labyrinth of fault lines. The land is the color of untanned leather. It shows repeated scars of vulcanism and exaggerated weather. It folds into tender pink places and stands up with dark, solitary towers of burnished lava. A strange and sexual beauty which keeps the eye alert and wandering.

The plateau has been harrowed by a drunken scholar. Demolished. Tumbled together. Rebuilt by an abstract bullet fired from the clouds. Even with the eyes covered, the landscape continues on inside the head. It refuses to turn off. The finality of this vastness keeps no origin private. Every man must mate bare naked with these sun-baked boulders. Each woman must come to grips with the edge. Every ocean, each star, all fragrant bodies of life are returned to pure electrical matter within this abyss.

The gorge is an emptying place. I feel small, taken by the suicidal—which we all possess. I shrink and exist as something missed by the eye, maimed in voice and hearing. Lips taste of metal, cold sweat, heated iron. Arms hold onto the body to keep it from flying. Above, the sky is a vagrant sea silvered with blue dust. Clouds cut along like razors. With each mark in my notebook a stone is loosened, words spill down the page and blind the eye with mirrored reflections of heaven.

Where the desert's coppery silence meets the lower edge of the sky there is an "acoustical" glow. A hawk dips in narrowing circles, casting its shadow upon the seared lip of a cinder cone. A distant thunderhead tells its story in paragraphs of rain. My body stands like a tree, branching with nerve endings—a musical keyboard upon which the wind composes its song. The eye is an inside-out auditory canal; the ear a giant picture window. In the mountain lion's footprint I see a roar. On a heated slab of stone my silhouette becomes a pulsing tower of music. It trembles like a black flower shuddering with electricity.

Hee hee hee heeeeeeee-e-e-e-e . . .

A canyon wren laughs in a descent of rapidly-fading crystalline notes. A honeybee buzzes by, stopping briefly to do a midair ballet for its mate. Far above, swallows dart and explode like the notes of Bartok on a transparent score. Hundreds of feet below, the river is serpentine and aglow, sharply contrasting with the eery blackness it has carved. Each syncline of textured stone is a musical sheaf, a text of resonating sound.

The water swings in, swings out, makes a foamy whirlpool and forms one, two, three little coves. In each of them pebbles tumble and clatter with a slightly different sound. Downstream, the Conscious River hits one solar-heated boulder after another, erupting in a steamy mist. Hazed by the spray, the black monoliths become sculptures by Maillol or Moore. Or, Paleolithic fertility goddesses: huge bellies, wide hips, giant breasts, wet mounds glistening with wild strands of moss.

There is a perfect mating of opposites here: fire, water; mist, stone. The dark, vertical, female gorge set within the bright, horizontal, male desert. In the canyon's booming hiss, in the vibrato interplay between sunlight and shadow, it is difficult to imagine the world being created by someone above or outside it. It is far easier to see the world emanating from sound; from a vibration produced by the sound itself—sound fragmenting into fire, water, air, earth.

•   •   •

Back in the truck I ponder the giant crack between the world above and the one below. The Conscious Gorge. High voltage of sound. Uneasiness of the edge. A vastness which commands my thirst. Ordinary language won't do. The hand struggles to jot a few notes, but is quickly made uneasy by a watchful buzzard tilting in a summer updraft. I twist the key in the ignition, rev the engine a few times, and try to avoid any more philosophic thinking. Across the plateau, the sky darkens. A rainbow thickens its flourescent arch. Then there are two, and a faint polarization of light into a third.

Within a mile I am off the road again, led astray by the rainbows. The windshield frames the black line of the desert gorge against the even gold of the plateau. The frightening geology which overpowered me moments ago is now safely enclosed in a rectangle of glass. The smell of sudden rain, the hot and cold wafts of the musky willow-bottom gorge, the remembrance of those steaming river-goddess boulders: all arouse me with an intoxicating, tingling high. I feel newly born, brought up from below, recomposed from giant skips of history. Perhaps I was once part of a lichen colony adhering to an iron-oxide stain on desert stone; or ethereal in identity; of liquid, mineral or escaping gas—now made human in a time-stopped increment of lightning flash.

Andale!

The gears are engaged once more. A rutted road leads back to the main pavement. The earth is a masterpiece of wetted architecture, smoke, frothing waves, flame. Thunderheads have fanned above, rumbling out deerhoof-patter of rain. Through the windows comes a steady flute-song of cold air. I am in an ark, riding a musical reef, a translucent syllable drifting through the open, alchemical text of time. The landscape glitters; it arrives; it disappears the moment it reaches the eye. The highway zigzags the rim of the gorge, then leaves it: Conscious Gorge; innocent birth of furor; immense opening of the terribly visible and transfixed.

Tonight, when I pull off to sleep, when I am alone or arrive home to my loved one and tangle in her flesh, then the numberless creation I witnessed today will come back. It will wear no mask but will linger in the soul's deepest recess. It will leave its mark as a monumental, uncharted garden—opaque and cherished; ephemeral and transparent. When I dream, it will be of the beginning of time. When I awake, it will be with two palms timidly outstretched to praise the derelict beauty of the universe.

I watched the wheel slow down, its painted figures whirling into focus . . .

IN THE DESERT WE DO NOT COUNT THE DAYS

I spent the night in a small hotel in a city not too far over the border. It was on an avenue lined with skimpy trees, always dusty from blowing sand. The place was painted pink and lime, filled with furniture left over from the forties. Off the lobby, in the bar, a man in a cocked felt hat served double tequilas under a portrait of Pancho Villa. Behind him a murky aquarium bubbled. It was hardly ample for the three enormous goldfish that prowled its waters. Sometimes a stray wanderer—an expatriate from Europe or the States—would nestle into the thick red leather of a bar stool and drink himself dizzy, pondering the slow, symbolic movements of the goldfish in the swampy water. But mostly the hotel's patrons were Mexican. Businessmen, occasional honeymooners, a visiting soccer team, a laborer and his family in from the thornbrush for dental work.

Close to the hotel was the Oficina de Correos, the telegraph house, and the Mercado Central—where one could drink iced alfalfa juice or papaya milkshakes and cool off from the desert heat under awnings strung with ribboned amulets. Just up from the market, the big circular roof of the bus station erupted with hieroglyphic puffs of diesel exhaust. Night and day, buses arrived and departed. Huge growling machines—decorated with yellow arrows and gold stars—carried a vagabond assortment of passengers across the purple desert to Guadalajara, Mexico City or further still into the coastal jungles of Veracruz and Oaxaca. Revving engines, the acrid smell of exhaust, the hurry of passengers, the *tinng-tinng* of ice-cream bells; the air of movement was constant. I had a special affection for the place. It reminded me that the world was much larger than I suspected.

The hotel rooms were built over squeaky stairways trellised with morning glories. Doves cooed in the palms. Weeping willows arched their graceful branches over a swimming pool in the courtyard. Giant boat-tailed grackles inhabited the lower reaches of these willows. When they flew into the foliage they became invisible, so that the trees themselves seemed to be talking, gossiping with hundreds of voices.

Sometimes, when two lovers walked arm in arm up to their room and pulled their blinds, the guests lounging about the pool would smile over the gentle creaking of the veranda above, a creaking which would gradually intensify and mix with the calls and sputtering whistles of the grackles. The whole world would be in motion. Balcony would sway, room would sway, trees would bob up and down, clouds would pause overhead, doves would circle the pool twice and return to their roosts.

An hour later the lovers would descend from their nest, sit by the pool, hold hands in their lounge chairs, and sleep a little. They never wandered far from their room, preferring to have it close when passion again overcame them. The grackles, too, remained close to their nests, never flying far from the weeping willows—their preference being to stay put, to chatter, to drink from the pool, and exercise their tongues.

For the hotel manager, the visitors, the maids and janitors, the lovers were neither amusing nor embarrassing, the birds neither a nuisance nor a novelty. They were all just another part of daily Mexican life. A round of gunfire, a coughing motorbike, a wild guitar crackling over a badly-connected loudspeaker would also be in place. There was a strange and fascinating order to these seemingly un-orchestrated sounds and doings, a chaotic rhythm that crept in and out of the body, leaving a tingle of color in nerve endings that hadn't been watered since birth. Mexico ruffled the flesh and stimulated the spine. It was a kind of chiropractor that aligned the senses to bring one down on all fours again, like a child. Here, new oxygen filled the brain. Life began to soar once more, above the woes of the mind.

Next to the hotel was an eatery called El Hombre Invisible—The Invisible Man Cafe. I ordered a breakfast of coffee, sweet rolls and cheese. A radio played, the sidewalks had been wetted by the street-sweepers, a musician slept by a newspaper man's kiosk. The early morning sun bounced its rays from the cafe's vermilion floors to the sulfur walls and blue ceiling. Everywhere there was decoration: Christmas bulbs, tinsel, paper cutouts of laughing skulls. Murals covered the rear wall: birds, fish, strange ark-like vessels riding whitecaps into a brilliant sunset. El Hombre Invisible was famous for these murals. My favorite was the one for which the cafe was named. It portrayed the outline of a man and within that outline was a set of bright yellow bones, a skeleton laced with vines growing up the legs and between the rib cage. A sun, moon and couple of macaws surrounded the invisible man. Two winged angels watched over him, bent in meditation.

I asked the owner of the cafe—a thin man with a clubfoot—for an explanation of the murals, and the name of the eatery. I thought the name might have been inspired by H.G. Wells. But he rebuked my theory.

"No, no. It is all out of my own past. Something that happened to me when I was just a boy. I looked into the mirror once. I was about five years old. To my amazement I could see right through myself. It wasn't my imagination, just something I happened to catch with my eyes. A glance of my bones, yellow bones in a blue shadow. After that, I believed I was invisible. I held that moment inside me for years without having the opportunity to express it in some way. Then when my father died and left me this little eating place, I thought: This is mine, I can do anything I please with it. So I started by repainting it. The whole place was just a dump, a shambles. After closing hours when everybody was asleep I began to paint the invisible man. Nothing calculated, you understand. I just picked up the brushes and let them move. That childhood moment was still with me and I thought: I want *everybody* to see it. After the mural was up on the wall, I changed the cafe's name—and that got people, all kinds, interested. They began to come in, admire the paintings, order a soda or a plate of refried beans and sausage. The place was one big painting, a story they could sit down inside of and relax. Little by little I am adding to the story—and I am going to keep painting just to find out how it all might end. If there ever is an end."

A young woman got up from her chair between the two angels and the invisible man. She was in place there, looking as if she'd stepped right out of the painting.

"You call those angels," the cafe owner went on to explain, "but 'angels' is not exactly the word. They are little women with wings. I put the wings on them to show that they are not quite of this world; that they are connected to a world beyond. Who knows that world? Perhaps the one they belonged to before they were born into this one. You see how they are bent down, as if looking for something? They are expressing their search for a lost or invisible world. The one we do not always remember because we are too busy with our problems, or work, or things of circumstance—like not having money, or a house to call your own, or someone to sleep with."

Customers wandered in and out. The clubfooted man returned to his cooking. The smell of chopped *cilantro* and spiced *mole* saturated the air. The radio played a soap opera. I ate in silence. The musician who had been sleeping by the new kiosk sauntered in, chose a corner table, ordered raw egg in orange juice, drank it down, and raised both arms high to the ceiling. At this the proprietor came over and whispered to me: "Now there is a man who *knows*." I looked at the musician, whose bulky frame was backed by the mural, whose rotund, whiskered head was surrounded by brightly-painted macaws. "What do you play?" I asked.

"Violinist!" he exclaimed, and proudly pointed to his case. "First, a man of the streets, then of the heart, then of God—after that, a violinist." Again he threw his arms to the ceiling as if to bless the little cafe. He clenched his fists to his chest, laughed and stood for a moment to sing:

> "*Por qué canto?*
> *Maybe because I'm a child of God.*
> *Maybe because I was born in the broken streets.*
> *Maybe because I am a spark from a little fire.*
> *Or perhaps because, like the flowers,*
> *I am filled with song . . .*"

He took his fiddle from its case and when he began to play the whole place lit up with the fire of his strings. Floor and ceiling joined colors, the bones in the mural danced in their blue outline, the cafe owner slapped his tortillas to the rhythm of the *violinista's* song. And that was how I began the morning that day. I paid my bill, tipped the musician, returned to the cool lobby of the hotel, drank a lime fizz, and watched the heated pall of dust from the desert lift and spread across the city's bushy skyline. The desert! Omnipresent, forever encroaching upon man's haphazard array of pavement and buildings and political bribings. Gently sifting its scouring sands upon the tilted kiosks and cement monuments that stood in the middle of traffic circles and oleander gardens.

Quietly, the hotel manager pondered his littered desk, fetal-like, bent over a pile of yellowed news clippings and archeological monographs. At first meeting he seemed reserved, rather stern. But he quickly thawed, revealing an underlying gentleness, a wry sense of humor and a good-natured wit. He was an unschooled scholar, a native of Cuauhtémoc—where the high desert rolls into wheat fields and wooded hills of the Sierra Madre. He once served in the Merchant Marines, married a girl from San Diego, lived in the States for awhile, then returned to the Mexican desert.

"Ah, San Diego," he chuckled, removing his thick eyeglasses to massage his pupils. "They eat so well there, and hardly ever smile. They drive so fast, and never ride together. And such an abundance of road signs! Every twenty minutes there's a green freeway marker reminding you how far you've come and how far to go. It seems the more advanced the society, the more information people need to get where they need to be."

I loved to hear him speak. He went on and on in bilingual paragraphs, a hedged maze intersecting, parting, opening into scattered points of light. His speech kaleidoscoped in and out with explosive roars followed by soft lulls and long pauses of thought. It was a relief from the monochrome, mercantile English of the States, a language fit to do business in but difficult for those fascinated by rhythm and meter.

Señor Alvarez, the hotel manager, was in his late seventies, had a few missing teeth, kept his face cleanly shaven, wore a wide tie printed with Mayan glyphs over a perpetual white shirt, and had a ring on his left hand in the shape of an ankh. The core of his philosophy was: "If you want to find true direction, first get good and lost."

He had a great collection of world maps. None of them showed political boundaries, only physical relief, oceanic trenches, hogbacks, evaporated lakes, climatic isobars and crisscrossed routes of famous cyclones. Above his desk, on dusty shelves, were assorted crystals, pottery shards, the poetry of Lorca, Neruda, Sor Juana and Rilke. Higher up was a set of *Wonder Books* picturing Neanderthal skulls, Incan masonry, Pygmy ladies tattooing their husbands, extinct birds in Mexican codices, Javanese shadow puppets, Altamira cave art, a bearded Ainu shaman.

Below his desk were folders containing papers about earthquakes, sundogs, igneous intrusions, cinder cones and the movement of glaciers. There were pictures of the constellations according to the way the Navajo, Papago and Huichol Indians saw them. To one side of his desk, piled high, almost to the level of the singing lazul finches in their bamboo cage, was a dusty stack of *The World at Home*, a twenty-two volume shopping guide to the planet's oddities. If you wanted to know something about the copulation of Amazon parrots, what an orangutan does for lunch, or why the Dalai Lama has big ears—it was all there under the singing birds.

referred to them only after visiting a site. "I like to see a place without knowing too much about it, to walk around, observing the slant of sunlight, the direction of the watersheds, the mounds and depressions. When I come back to my desk I go over what I've seen, figure out where I've been. My mind becomes like a spotlight, rotating across a dark ocean at night. It picks out a few luminous islands, and those are the ones I make note of—to ponder, to explore.

"I prefer to go beyond what historians have chosen to give us, what they *think* has happened, or what they have selected to remember as important. Then I come forward, linking what is common to all cultures beneath the surface. Little by little I work my way towards the mouth of the cave, and suddenly I step out into the light of the present. It's like walking out of a dream, where all things are fused, transposed, sorted, transformed."

One lazy afternoon, the temperature near 100, and a great overhead fan slowly churning away, Señor Alvarez elaborated on

Hortencio Ortiz, the owner of the Invisible Man Cafe. "Why, he's a self-made folk artist. He went around most of his life in poverty. No mother, a sick father who died an early death of tuberculosis, a bunch of brothers who crossed the line as wetbacks and never returned. He was just a starving cripple with no beans in his belly. Then one day he inherited the cafe. Suddenly in the middle of his loneliness, his chaos, things took hold. He bought paints, started in on the walls, didn't give a damn what people were saying. The murals took shape. Newspapers interviewed him. Someone in the States printed an article on him. Tourists showed up and the place was endorsed. Now he gets all types: locals, street people, policemen, secretaries, even the city mayor."

The hotel manager took a gulp of iced coffee, and handed me a newspaper. "Look, let me show you someone else, self-taught like Hortencio Ortiz. He's a potter, lives far out in the desert. Flaviano Campos—a good man. Very well known in big cities in your country, and a guy worth taking the trouble to look up. Why don't you? I'll draw you a map. It's a few hours south of here and into the hills a bit."

The newspaper article showed a picture of Campos cutting a lock of his daughter's hair to fashion a paintbrush with which to decorate his pottery. Another photo brought out the designs on his ceramics— a curious blend of his own style with that of prehistoric peoples who lived in canyon bottoms near his village. But my real incentive to visit Flaviano Campos was the hotel manager's enthusiasm.

"Look at this pot," he smiled, lifting a feather-light ceramic from a shelf at the rear of his office. The bowl was covered with a sawtooth design, painted with fine black lines of manganese slip zigzagging in optical illusions. "The man is a genius. Curators have him spotted. They've got his work in Chicago and New York. Collectors are trying to get him to move to Juarez or El Paso to make his work more accessible. But he refuses to move. He has a secret mine of clay in the hills. And he loves his village. As a kid he'd tend cows with his grandfather and pick up shards in the cactus. He imitated their designs in the wet clay of river washes. Then he taught himself how to make tablets and platters. Soon he was coiling rolls of clay into bowls. He lives right on an old trade route. One that used to take merchants all the way from Tenochtitlán to Pueblo Bonito, up in New Mexico.

"Behind his village are the remains of a market center where traders kept live macaws in clay cages, and shells and turquoise in thick-walled depositories. The ruins are melting away now. Anthropologists have catalogued them and taken away most of the findings. But Flaviano they've overlooked. He's there in the desert keeping alive that old-style pottery. In fact, I believe he's making thinner, better pots than the ancients who inspired him. Look at this pot, just look! No wheel, no kiln. It's fired in a wire basket over cow chips. He buys no paints, no clay, no brushes, nothing. It's all from his mind, his hands, the earth."

The next day I drove out through the city's junkyards and barrios to the desert. Tatters of wash hung over rusty clotheslines and thorn scrub. Thieves markets were spread with auto fenders, dirty transmissions, hood ornaments, rolls of jagged wire, rope, pvc pipe. A small tienda selling cokes and popsicles was built into the fuselage of a crashed airplane. A roadside cross marked the spot of someone's fatal accident. Then, nothing. Only a lavender stretch of sand, a gray pall of dust closing in. Not a bird. Not a single leaf. Only the hot, dry tongue of the desert licking in mad flashes at the mind. The road went blurry. Creosote plants assumed the shapes of ghosts. An oncoming bus hogged both lanes, its one wobbly cyclops headlight flashing through the blowing sand. Other than that there was hardly a vehicle on the pavement. For three hours dust sandpapered my windshield. The wipers melted against the glass.

When the wind halted and the blacktop petered out, I found

myself on a gentle rise of hills, slowly dropping into windbreaks of pink tamarisk and cottonwoods hugging a dry creekbed. Then began the green patches of dry-farmed wheat and alfalfa. There was an excuse of a village here: a stone church with its steeple missing, a dirt square with two iron benches under flowering trees, a little bingo stand set up under a striped awning by a solitary lamppost. On one bench sat three elderly men in white shirts; on the opposite bench, three elderly women in all black. A group of children gathered around a giant roulette wheel at the bingo stand. I approached, bet a peso on a red square, and watched the wheel slow down, its painted figures whirling into focus: humpback, cactus, mermaid, frog, owl, and finally the peacock. Luck having it, my peso was tripled. From the change in my pocket I added to my win. I bought a can opener from the same bingo stand; and a beer. Bands of flamboyant light shot up from the hills where the sun had dropped. To the east a half-moon rose over an uneven volcanic fault line.

I was informed that Flaviano Campos lived close by, in a tiny settlement of about twenty-five families—part of an old hacienda that had been returned to the people during the days of Pancho Villa. A couple hours of twilight remained. I lingered for a while, then took a dusty, pock-marked road out of the village. I drove slowly, the automobile definitely out of place. Children on burros laughed and deliberately blocked the way to keep me from passing. Irrigation water crossed the road and gurgled lazily into apple orchards. Tin cans jingled on strings between cactus fences to keep the blackbirds away. Rural sounds magnified from miles around. A farmer unloading tools from a cart, the crack of someone splitting kindling wood, an electrical generator beginning its *putt-putt-putt*, donkeys in off-chorus brays, dogs yelping, kids laughing or crying (but never a mother's reprimand or a scold).

A bit farther, a little darker, and I began to get nervous. Where was this guy Campos? Everyone had a different set of directions to offer.

"*Sí*, up over that hill, cross the llano, past the sawmill." Or, "*Por allá*, cross the field in front of the hacienda ruins, then along the wash following the cottonwoods." Everyone was extremely friendly. "Stay with us, have some fresh tortillas and goat cheese. Are you rushing? Night is falling. Refresh yourself. It's peaceful here. Why hurry?"

Something of the city remained in me, though. I hadn't been in the desert long enough for it to wear off. It was that odd, proud determination to make Flaviano's by nightfall. On schedule. *Schedule!* Under such a sky, such a moon, in such a timeless spot! As darkness hit, I found myself aimlessly driving the llano's dry expanse—no sign of village lights; only the fat, lopsided moon, bearded with the haze of the desert. There, in that lilac splendor, I remembered the words of Señor Alvarez: "First get good and lost." A few minutes later, an old Ford pickup approached, water cans banging in its bed, a broken muffler sputtering. A bearded young man and his pregnant wife sat behind a huge steering wheel. "Ah, Campos. Sure. I know him. You are real close. Follow me. I can lead you right to his door."

Over the llano, not even bothering to switch our headlights on, we bumped along, twisting down into an arroyo, through a herd of dappled horses, and in fifteen minutes—no problem at all—arrived in Flaviano Campos' village. His was an adobe house, like all the others: flat roof, unplastered, a few coriander plants and two drums of water near the stone doorsteps. I was greeted by Señora Campos, a slight woman in a plain dress, hair pulled back, a youthful smile on her dark face. She was in the middle of ironing, her children spread around her catching a few scribbled images on the tv (even here!). Flaviano, a small, handsome, bright-eyed man was busy in his workroom adding the final touch to a set of commissioned pots enroute to Arizona for a collector. After a round of formal greetings, some strong, sweetened coffee and a few tortillas, he began to loosen up and talk shop.

"This commissioned stuff! *Pos*, I don't enjoy it so much. It's a problem. I can use the money, why not. But I lose so much time on this, I'm not doing what I really want to do. You see these thick lines I am applying? They are what the man wanted, but they are not me. My style is thin lines, very thin lines. The hair-at-the-tip-of-the-brush kind, *sabes*? Here, look at this pot. This is what I made when I had more time, when no one knew me. I'd begin putting down these fine lines and by the end of the decoration I'd be transported to places I never dreamed of. All because of the lines!

"When collectors didn't come to bother me I had all the time I wanted to go off by myself and to collect clay. And I could spend another few days in the fields plowing and planting and letting new designs come to me. I used to trade my pottery for clothes for my family in thrift shops across the border. Or sell them in hotels in El Paso and then buy tractor parts. Now people make all sorts of money offers, and dictate what I'm to create. 'Oh, I saw one of your pots at the museum and I want one just like it. Here let me write you a check.' But I have decided that no matter how much money they offer, I must resist. What I'm working on now will the the last of my commissions. I must return to my own designs and take chances. Like when I first began. What's in store for me if I become too secure? A soft bed, a full tank of gas? No rough edges, no stumbles and experiments and fresh ideas?

"You know, whenever I leave this place my head begins to hurt. I get to Juarez or El Paso, or even as far north as Albuquerque, and I am like an animal without a watering tank. Thirsty for home. I cross back over the line and raise my arms toward heaven and say, 'I'm free!' Perhaps not 'free' by your standards, but in my poverty I am not a rushed man. I look at people in cities and while they ware talking they seem to be elsewhere. Planning what to do next. And they always seem to take the long way around to do what they need to do. Here in my village we are not so involved in abstractions. We turn the earth, rake it, put in the seed. Hoe, water and harvest. You might be surprised because I own that pickup out there, or a tractor, or a tv— but they are not intrusions or distractions. They are modern things I can use or misuse. Like the land, the mesquite wood, the horse. I can use or misuse them."

Flaviano returned to his brush strokes, joked a bit with his children, and after an hour's work pushed his pottery aside, covered it with a soft cloth, popped a Tecate for each of us and resumed conversation. "I'll tell you what bothers me. It's that these creations of mine have suddenly become 'art.' That is to say they are different and in demand. But why does it work this way? That I should find myself in the position of turning out pots less my own with less time put into them, and all the while prices soaring? I don't think it should work that way. I won't let it. I think I'll return to producing fewer bowls and keep the prices affordable. Or perhaps the prices should be so high that people won't approach me at all. Then I'll have all the time in the world."

At this Flaviano Campo's wife looked up from her ironing with a beaming smile, "—and maybe we will make a second honeymoon!"

We talked until the moon was low. Flaviano offered to show me a camp spot under his favorite cottonwood down the arroyo behind the house. "Would it be too much trouble?" I asked, more out of politeness than sincerity. "Trouble? Trouble! Do we have time for trouble out here, dear?" The potter and his wife laughed heartily, got up from their chairs, rustled up some blankets, tossed everything into their pickup, and down the arroyo we went. A small fire was lit, my bed was laid out, and an owl hooted casually, securing its territory.

"In the desert we do not count the days," Señor Campos mused. "Or at least we didn't before the collectors came," his wife added. They smiled and stirred the sand with their fingers. "Yes, I suppose. During the harvest season I took the sickle, happy to be there with only the sun as my timepiece. While I worked, a thousand ideas from God, himself, entered my head. When the grain and *calabazas* were put away, I gathered clay and set to molding it. All the designs on my pots—they are gifts from nature. I am not to be credited. Here, look.

Credit these trees, this fire! The patterns between the flames, the dark and light shapes of the moving leaves. Museums may say what they want, naming my pots and classifying them and comparing them to other cultures. But it is all so second hand.

"At first I thought, *bueno*—let them call me what they want as long as they like pots and want to own them. But then they wanted to shake my hand. They wanted me to appear with my pots, to say something. And what could I say in Chicago or Scottsdale that they could understand? Not many comprehend the solitude it takes for nature to enter your mind, and work itself out again. Collectors have this notion that they are helping me, that money makes me happy. They don't know that the time I lose on my crops and the money I make off my commissions buys food that doesn't taste the same or fill me up like the food I grow myself. And I have to be stubborn about all this. I don't make a satisfactory pot on a dissatisfied stomach. Businessmen come with great propositions. 'Flaviano, why don't you put the village to work? Someone could excavate the clay, someone could mold the pots, someone could prepare the slips, and you could do the design. Work less, increase production, make more profit.'

"And I reply, 'Oh sure. And who would grow the food? Who would tend the animals? Who would open and close the irrigation canals? The village would spend all its profits driving to the border obtaining food which they used to grow!' And we go round and round. There are merchants who think they can get me to make more pots and sell them at lower rates. Every time they proposition me like that I *raise* the prices. With the price of food in the market these days, if we all stopped raising beans and became artists then we'd have to sell our wares at extravagant prices. So that ends it. The merchants bump away in their little automobiles angry and defeated."

Flaviano threw another stick of mesquite on the fire. "It's moments like we're sharing right now that we like to have time for. To tell our stories, to speak our truths. To remember the day and still be alive to the fullest for night. I'm still working the fields and rounding up the cows as I did when I was a boy. After that, there's the pottery. The work, the play, the lazy moments like these, they are necessary to ripen ideas. I find my designs in nature, away from the distractions of the human world. My pots are nothing I went to art classes for, nothing I learned from books. I think it's best that way. Natural."

It was almost dawn when we said goodnight. A breeze played through the heart-shaped cottonwood leaves, carrying sweet scents of blossoming tamarisk. Sleep filled me, beckoning like a magnet, a hand from winged muse reaching from the Milky Way. I was a tiny raft in the sand, a hollow outline filling with light. I remembered the violinist's song, the wisdom of the hotel manager behind his cluttered desk, the grackles and doves by the pool, the dancing outline of bones on the wall of the Invisible Man Cafe, and the long drive through a veil of silver dust to get to "this" world from "that."

She eyed me intensely, at once with desire and apprehension. The rainbow in the west evaporated . . .

LA VIRGEN DE
GUADALUPE

S he was dark, *morena*, and she used to serve me the daily special
   at Clancy's Eat, just along South 285. She came from a migrant
family. We used to speak Spanish. I had a crush on her, but almost
deliberately I kept her in an unattainable place—a little frustrating
from both sides, I suppose. And yet, that thin edge between us kept
each encounter rather electric, mysterious and rich with unfinished
conversations.

Our talk was always about life lived simply as opposed to life made
complicated. Sometimes, when there was no business and the proprietor took off to purchase ground round or chips in town, we'd sit at
the same table and talk and maybe make a few passes. "We will talk
maybe more at the drive-in, sometime?" But I never took her up on
it. And when I got to know her better she admitted she was only half-
serious. "I would rather you come with me to San Ignacio," she once
said. "I would show you our humble ranch, the chickens, the oats, the

two milk cows, the rabbits. And we have a beautiful spring. I have always thought the water to be miraculous, like stories I've heard of Fatima."

The next time I saw her I would have maps in my hand, we would scan them—or at least I would. And her hand would sometimes be touching mine—just the side of the hand, very slightly. We would talk about Barranca de Cobre, that immense canyon all multicolored with tiny black pines in its bottom, not far from where she lived in the Sierra Madres. But only once did we ever get beyond the doors of Clancy's Eat.

There was a rainbow in the west, over the Guadalupes. The early-morning sun was a gentle spotlight through the violet clouds, thunderheads parting after an all-night electrical storm. I looked at Reina, truly a child, a princess. "I am going to El Paso, why not come? We can cross over to Juarez, see the big cathedral, enjoy the market, listen to the street musicians and even eat real mangoes." She eyed me intensely, at once with desire and apprehension. The rainbow in the west evaporated—that *arco-iris* that shone like a corona above her head. She had only a few words, coyly spoken: "I cannot leave my job. And even so, my parents would find out that I went with you."

From that point on, assured that we would never come together in anything more than casual talk at Clancy's Eat, I turned precariously toward mythologizing my relationship with this child-woman whose name meant "queen." Every conversation became a painting. I would stretch a new canvas. I would write a poem. I would take my brush and paint Reina opening the pages of an immense book, dark and mysterious. From the book arose a word—part Spanish, part Hebrew, part Sanskrit. And from the word arose a humble farmhouse with glowing lamps in each window, a red cow, and hillcocks of green oats. In the sky I painted a rainbow; under the rainbow, a spring. And a white dove singing from the waters, singing a word back into Reina's open book.

But one day Reina wasn't at Clancy's. The whole family had been taken back across the line in one of those government vans, the green ones with barred windows. She never had a chance to see the paintings I painted nor the poems that spoke the course of my fantasy regarding the places we went and the affair—mystical, allegorical—that Reina and I shared.

Since then I have not gone back to Clancy's Eat. I know there is a white woman that works there now; I have heard that she is "reliable." And that she takes no breaks to look at rainbows in the west, nor does she sit with customers to talk about miraculous springs or great crevasses cutting through the bowels of the earth. I have not exaggerated. In fact, I have not told enough. And I am glad for that, for the silence that withholds the exact details of the source to the aloof and aloft direction that my work has taken over this past year.

Is it not this way, so much of the time? That a moment's crossing—a face with a rainbow for a crown, lit by the rising sun; or a fleeting voice in a light as pale as the first crescent moon—should determine the course of one's life and work, should reveal a fiber, a bone, a fossil, an artifact overlooked; or awaken from the unconscious a series of illuminated scrolls, each with a picture, a landscape, a story or a song yet to be told? So much time we take to arrive at conclusions through books and speculation; yet such vast and concise pictures present themselves in a single instant to be shared with another human being, perhaps never to be seen again.

There are times, many moments, when I think back on those two hands turned flat on the table, barely touching, at Clancy's. It's a simple enough story. I am glad for what I have been able to tell. For the maps, the electrical storm, and for what is there, awakened, still left inside me to be sung.

The whisssssst-whup-whutter of mammal bodies rains upon the landscape like little flicks of a delicate chisel on a Japanese woodblock.

THE MAKING OF SOUND
VISIBLE THROUGH
SILENCE

C arlsbad Caverns. The still, dark air just before dawn. At one end of the sky a hint of illumination but not enough to matter yet. I approach the landscape like a person deprived of eyesight. Feeling my way through the darkness. Aware of every texture, smell, and sound. The changing air currents. The aeolian notes of a pre-dawn breeze meandering through prickly pear and wiry branches of ocotillo. Flutter and chirp of feathered creatures picking through the underbrush. A waft of guano. Damp sumac. Campfire smoke on my own clothes.

In the heavens a single planet scintillates like fire, thickens its glow into a gloaming vibration. For the first time in years I do not remember anything I tried to learn about that planet: its name, magnitude, when it rises or sets. The silence here makes me forget, gives me a new shape in the heavens upon which to meditate. That fiery planet is simply a note, an anonymous but powerful keynote in the song of quiet worship as I sit at the edge of the caverns waiting for morning.

OOOOOOoooooo—o o o o o . . .

Is the earth yawning in this blackness? I hear a deep, bellowing sigh, delicate at first, then baritone in pitch. Accompanying it is a rich and potent draft. Without seeing the cavern entrance, I know it is near. I hear its voice. I am aware of an opening in the earth. I smell its inner muscle. I know that if I enter I could get lost forever.

Swallows now, in upward, reverse vortex. They are barely visible in the darkness, but I *feel* their flight, the swift breeze created by their sudden flocking, spiraling, lifting. Their little cheeps and chatters sound like many unoiled winches all squeaking at once. Such a pathetic comparison! A reminder of the world of machines I occupy so much of the time.

There is another sound in this silence, too. It makes my eyes work hard in the blackness. Something seems to be raining, but it is not rain. Something is audible from above, falling—and I am struggling to *see* what it might be. It is not until there is enough light that I realize what this heavenly resonance is. Dawn has fully kindled the sky; the sun is a red slit on the horizon. I can *see* the sound now. The air is suddenly teeming with hairy, brown acrobats that were there in the dark all the time—just as they've been for the past sixty million years. But I must strain a bit to glimpse the details of this massive fluttering sound. When at last my eyes are able to focus, I discern hundreds of thousands of Mexican Free-tailed Bats zeroing in on the caverns after a night of feeding. They've been out since last twilight, funnelling upward above the limestone canyons, high above the cave opening into the pink air above the Pecos River, filling their bellies full of moths—never once touching down.

This morning the *whissssst-whup-whutter* of mammal bodies rains upon the landscape like little flicks of a delicate chisel on a Japanese woodblock. Each chip flies into the air as a mark is made, and in turn seems to reproduce another mark—a continuous birth of action-made-into-sound-made-into-visible-fragments of a great alphabet: 500,000 letters worth.

Whissssst-whup-whutter . . .

    Whissssst-whup-whutter . . .

It is a sound much more powerful than the action of the swallows, because of the sheer numbers creating it. Imagine half a million bats circling the landscape, then tucking in their wings a thousand feet above their home—the caverns—and suddenly letting their bodies whistle and flap as they free-fall toward their mark. Once inside the darkness they do a flip, all very precise, and perch upside down, 250 or more to the square foot.

The effect of these tightly-packed mammal bodies flying above, suddenly descending toward the horizon, is like a film of smoke run backwards—so that what you perceive is a great smudge in the air, thousands of bats reversing themselves as a single multitude—downward into the narrow vent of a giant limestone womb.

Add the twitter of a mockingbird against the breaking dawn, and the shape of a mule deer's head between a cluster of cactus, and you have yet another dimension to play on the senses. The deer stares motionless, absorbing your slightest move—the flick of an eyelash, the bob of an Adam's apple, even the tiny hairs on your arm which lift in the dawn breeze. And the mockingbird's erratic song—it replicates all of the movements I have thus far mentioned: the upward spin of swallows; the downward plunge of bats; the motion-less gaze of the doe; the rising sun; the fading gloam of the nameless planet; the north-to-south movement of clouds as they break and scatter to let the morning through.

The first People must have had a word for all of this—the making of sound visible through silence. They must have had a word also for the Mexican Free-tailed Bat: that furry, winged creature that falls from the sky at dawn into the mouth of the earth with a *whutter* and a *whirr*.

I was here, I observed, I created; I witness the rising sun, my body feels its warmth, my hands give thanks.

DESERT GRAFFITI

Years ago the site was undeveloped. It couldn't be located on maps. It bore no name save for the one known only to the prehistoric people who hunted and gathered here and passed away. It remained a mysterious spot deep within a fissured maze of lava flow at the base of a snowy peak rising high above New Mexico's southern desert. You found your way there by asking around: a ranch hand, a hay baler, a fire lookout headed up a switchback in a pickup full of melting groceries. Usually the reply would be: "Oh yeah, just follow the Three Creeks road until you ford the forks. Park where the rocks turn real black and walk up the south-facing canyon to your right. Go about two miles into the lava until you start to see the 'high-row-glyphs' on the second tier of rock just above your head to the left."

But word got around. One person told another over the decades until the directions reached the wrong ears. Off-road vehicles managed to get into places that people had formerly only found by foot.

Hordes of vandals came searching for Indian pots, shards, arrowheads, metates, turquoise beads and pictographs left by desert dwellers a thousand years back. They found these things and they took them. Some were put into trunks and lost. Others were sold and resold for a hefty profit among non-Indian history buffs. A fraction of the artifacts—a tiny percentage of a percentage—ended up in museums for public benefit. A large majority returned into dust after a profitable exchange had been made.

Then came the pickups, 4x4s, jacked up and with chrome roll bars and double rows of spotlights. On their translucent-pink bug deflectors were stencilled the in-fashion names with which their owners had christened them: "Animal," "War Machine," "Miss Fit." In their beds were portable generators and jackhammers. Hundreds of symbolic designs intricately carved by Indian hunters, storytellers, shamans and astronomers, were power-chiseled—lichens and all—right off the cliffsides. Some of the vandals took potshots at the faces they saw there: the penetrating eyes, the lithe shapes of prancing bucks, the dancing outlines of masked figures. Some guilt no doubt, remained in the vandal's genes. A subconscious spasm moved their triggers. Perhaps they didn't know what they were shooting at or why, but they fired nevertheless. Their bullets ricocheted from the mystical eyes and prancing quadrupeds on the rock facade before them. Their shots revealed a hidden need to do away with even the slightest trace of the people their forefathers had slain as Europe colonized the American West. As the new settlers decimated the original inhabitants of the land, so did they decimate the hunters' and gatherers' intimate knowledge of it; their sense of balance with nature; the science of their medicine, agriculture, and architecture.

Now the site is developed—what is left of it, anyway. A substantial road leads into the lava flow. Parks-and-Recreation signs make sure you don't get lost. The main outcrop of petroglyphs is enclosed by chain-link fencing. A paved trail gets you started up the slope. Metal tags explain the shrubbery along the way. Portable toilets and picnic tables in a graveled parking-lot have been half-burned and defaced. Garbage cans overflow, fast-food refuse blows. Flies won't leave you alone. It's a favorite spot for weekenders and one most serious campers completely avoid. There is no permanently-employed ranger. There is no part-time guide to explain even the slightest history of the makers of the rock art. The public swallows the line that hiring such employees would take too much tax money from their pockets, when in reality the government gives priority to its over-inflated defense budget. Now that those who loyally shared directions to the secret site have seen what has become of it, perhaps they will second-think such divulgence of information in the future. Myself included.

In a different watershed, several hours north, there's another cluster of petroglyphs of note—some 14,000 lining a twenty-mile volcanic cliff of 200,000 year-old lava. Overlooking the vermillion waters of the silt-laden Rio Grande as it cuts through Albuquerque, this site has one of the finest collections of Native American petroglyphs in North America. Most of the rock art was pecked into the desert-varnished stone by the Anasazi Indians, ancestors of the modern Pueblo people, between the 14th and early 16th centuries. Turtles, snakes, spirit masks, stars, planets, cloud formations, anthropomorphic beings and geometrical abstractions of natural forms are among the designs represented. The entire escarpment is about to be turned into almost 13,000 acres of desert land managed by the National Park Service and the city of Albuquerque. Naturally, the land developers are upset.

"It's graffiti, that's all. Just like the graffiti we have on city buildings and underpasses in our own culture. 'Cept *their* culture is gone. Why preserve scribbles from a bunch of disappeared people that don't have anything to do with us?" That's how an enraged realtor described the Anasazi culture and its contribution to Native American rock art—an expression as unique and original as anything preserved in The Museum of Modern Art or in the great anthropological museums of Paris and Mexico City.

The realtor's investment property was undergoing an impact study by the State Archeology Department—an effort to determine the importance of certain ceremonial figures and clan symbols on a group of boulders, and whether they should be included in the rock-art preserve. Frustrated over both the idea that his land should be considered for purposes other than development, and the slowness of the archaeological study, the man hired a heavy-equipment operator to dislodge the boulders. In the middle of the night they were lifted into a truck, sacred etchings and all, and dumped in front of the Albuquerque city hall. This brazen statement was applauded by other developers, even though the man was cited, the boulders hauled back to their original site, and the property put under restriction. One can only sit nervously and await further vengeance, though: the deliberate mutilation of the rock art in its natural surroundings.

Land investors like the enraged realtor continue to badmouth the idea of an "art preserve." As the irreplaceable-cultural-resource argument pressures them into compromise, most agree that "a corner of the 13,000 acres in question should be preserved." But a majority see the delicate intaglios of human expression as mere curiosities in the way of "houses that need to be built for honest-working people like you and me." There are plenty of hikers, anthropologists, historians, artists, city-council members, and "honest-working people" that would argue differently. Not to mention the unanimous pro-preservation vote by Native Americans from Alaska to Tierra del Fuego:

"You worship indoors, we worship outdoors. Would you approve of a bulldozer cutting through a corner of Saint Patrick's or the Vatican to make way for frame-and-stucco tract homes? Do you think we approve the bulldozing of land that is sacred to us, that breathes with our ancestors presence?"

The inconsiderate hobbyists who loot prehistoric sites and the vandals who fire bullets at artistic, religious, or architectural monuments—whether cathedrals or kivas—are of the same breed who refuse kinship with cultures outside their own. Possessed of a volatile, short-wicked egocentricity, they exhibit a disconnectedness that okays the decimation of one people's past for the sake of a newcomer's present. Or, of one man's running over another's family for diversion or self-preservation.

These delicate intaglios of human expression, this "graffiti" boldly pecked into the dark oxides of desert stone is language of its own; is poetry, is human communication reaching farther back than the art of European colonists or Conquistadores. The age of the stone outcrops upon which the symbols are inscribed puts Moses and his tablets in the context of having existed only a couple minutes ago. Petroglyphs in the desert Southwest have been documented as far back as several thousand years. The supernatural, anthropomorphic figures suggest that their makers were in tune with their unconscious depths; that they saw into celestial realms; that they listened to voices deep beyond the surface strata of normal human communications.

The intricacy, magnitude and sophistication of the petroglyphs affirm that our interior world is at least as vast as our exterior one. Places seen in dreams are remembered as maps and take their places next to landscapes precisely observed in the waking world. Prehistoric hunters and gatherers of what is now New Mexico, and their present Pueblo Indian descendants found a system of symbolic expression—minimal lines to indicate maximum imagery— to adequately convey their Underworld experiences. The spirits and archetypal beings that inhabit the dark, collective self *speak* from the rocks on which they are carved. But they take their places next to intimately-recorded migration routes, clan symbols, location of water holes, and areas of plentiful game in the conscious, physical world, too. There is no division of time, no fragmentation of worlds. Only a blend, a balance.

I know of an escarpment in a box canyon in the upper reaches of the Chihuahuan Desert that I refuse to give directions to. A richly-patined upthrust of stone faces the eastern sunrise which—at a certain time of year—explodes through a canyon between two high peaks. One of these peaks violently erupted about 35,000,000 years ago, oozing molten aprons of lava that cooled and cracked into a black labyrinthine tangle. Walking through this tangle can be a surreal experience, especially after a powdering of January snow. Delicate bayonet-leafed sotol plants spire from the volcanic rock with sword-like stems. Orange colonies of lichen dazzle the eye from between melting shelves of ice. The head goes dizzy with a constant vibration set up by desert light bursting upon black volcanic blisters capped with snow banks. But the snow doesn't last long. Within a couple of days every trace of winter has disappeared. A dry season follows; and finally, summer showers. Neon-green ferns lace the pressure-buckled lava rifts. Sacred datura flowers open under the moon, attracting giant lunar moths. Lightning forks through the night sky. It is so clear, so quiet, you can hear a star touch the horizon as Earth turns.

Where the lava flow meets the crinkled, alluvial aprons that spread from Sierra Blanca, there's an ancient camp where I go to be alone. Everywhere, on glazed boulders, are petroglyphs left by prehistoric people. Humped-back fluteplayers do their primordial dance of awe, reproduction and erotic play. From their bug-like bodies rise giant phalli, equal in length and proportion to the flutes they blow into with their antennaed heads. The notes they play represent the music of social and sexual intercourse, the dance of insemination and birth that keeps the world turning. Pecked into the rocks alongside these bug-like fluteplayers are sun-headed beings birthing moons and planets. A fat cosmic divinity holds an all-seeing eye inside the circle of its belly. Or is it a bellybutton? Around the interior perimeters of its stomach are mountain ranges, a circular geometric fringe of peaks.

Before me, tumbled into narrow sandy arroyos, are black mono-liths etched with configurations that show the sophisticated imagi-nation of the artists that created them. They did some real magic with the line. They took the straight edge of a horizon and bent it into a perfect circle. A solar body. A sun. A moon. An all-seeing retina. The Earth. The galaxy. A ceremonial kiva. The interior of a home. A person's face. A spiral without beginning or end.

When an artist or storyteller halved a circular motif, he ended up with two arched rainbows. One right-side up, the other upside down. When he creased these rainbows into right angles, a series of terraces or steps was formed. Stairways leading back and forth between heaven and earth. Geometrical representations of lightning bolts. Rain-bearing thunderheads. The zigzag path of a snake. Ladders leading in and out of homes or underground religious chambers.

The Anasazi artists inscribed a cross within a circle. Not a Chris-tian cross, but one of equal lengths—dividing the circle into four seasons. A design to show intersection of vertical and horizontal realms: raindrops falling from heaven to meet earth's thirsty horizon; man's vertical shaft entering woman's horizontal body in the act of procreation. The shape of the great religious kivas replicated not only the eternal circle, but an abstraction of the womb's shape. And the womb's shape related back to that of the solar system. Some petro-glyphs had a simple dot at a circle's center—perhaps the open eye of all the permeating Creative Force. Or, a symbolic reminder of our own umbilical connection with Mother Earth.

The petroglyph is a map that rotates and unfolds into myriad dimensions; an exploding ideogram—tenseless, dream connected, associated with dance, music, a choreographed line of singers, sexual pleasure, the hunt, ritual magic, agriculture, pollination, celestial explosions, sidereal time, rain, lightning, eclipses, earthquakes, pro-creation. Men with stars for heads, planet bodies. Turtles, pumas, beetles, frogs, pollywogs, deer, coyote, bighorn sheep, butterflies, an exaggerated phallus, the upraised legs of a woman in the act of birth: all born from a single line, a horizon, a vertical rainstorm, a single snowflake, an earthbound streak of electricity, a heavenbound corn shoot expanding upward and outward like a child greening with life, raising its arms in praise.

There are countless numbers of horned personages, too. They have nothing to do with the Christian idea of Satan. Nor with the thoughtless "devil-worship" implications that misled religious fanatics have accused the Anasazis of—fanatics whose bullets have defaced hundreds of prehistoric spiral emergence-myth designs. Horns, as a part of ancient graphic symbolism, almost always—and universally— denote supernatural connections: shamanic power, a guardian totem, a beneficial spirit. These are different symbols from the stylized peckings meant to denote antlers of deer or elk, the curved horns of mountain sheep, the stubby pronghorns of antelope.

This ancient camp I describe has an area of reversed topography— a volcanic dike whose edges have been eroded away; a dark, sun-glazed wall a couple miles long. At the easternmost lip of this igneous facade are several carved handprints. Perhaps the old people meant to say "I was here, I offered my thoughts into the universe, I supplicated the gods for water and abundant crops, for wholeness among my people, for healthiness of the self and every plant and being it connects with." Perhaps the hands simply and spontaneously "signed" a site, signed a few adjoining petroglyphs the way an artist signs a canvas. "I was here, I observed, I created; I witness the rising sun, my body feels its warmth, my hands give thanks."

On an early winter's day I shared this spot with a cottontail rabbit and—in the impeccably-blue heavens above—a fighter plane performing mock reconnaissance.

Leaving a terrible sonic shock wave in its trail, the plane passed within a hundred feet of the lava dike, an American star painted on its triangular tail.* The rabbit scattered into the under branches of a creosote bush. At my feet a wedge of sand loosened from its miniature cirque and spilled into a sparkling waterfall. The back of my throat felt dry and scoured. I thought of the dramatic change in history that occurred at 5:29 on a July morning in 1945 just two ridges to the west: the explosion of the first atomic bomb. I shut my eyes and the ancients' handprints echoed in sound-pictures on the insides of my eyelids. I saw the crimson outline of the fighter's tail against a green sun. And floating shapes of petroglyphs, extravagant configurations in an infra-red zodiac.

I stood in a time-vacuum watching the ghosts of a vanished race reappear inside my head, hearing a distant scream of wind through wings. The fighter? A diving nighthawk? My senses refused to identify. In the anatomy of my muscles was the animal track, the stick figure, the deer, the lizard, the lightning bolt, the terraced thunderhead. Symbolically they floated, luminous phosphenes electrically pulsing through the arteries.

The body is a petroglyph made of brittle air and blood; of sunlight etched upon dark streaks of mineral-washed bone. The universe is a fragile empire dissolved on the tip of the tongue, a flaming syllable fluttering out deep from within.

* *Similar military maneuvers are responsible for the exfoliation of rock, and their valuable petroglyphs, in the Nevada Desert.*

Dogwolf was a totem identification with that part of me that seemed 'right' and couldn't say 'no.'

HOW MANY WAYS TO
TELL OF COYOTE?

A t precisely one minute after midnight on New Year's Eve, a
Coyote ran across the Pan American Highway in the high
beams of a Mexican bus. As we climbed into the desert highlands near
Zacatecas, the driver looked at the old man standing at his side who
was lighting his cigarettes and giving him coffee to ward off sleep
through the wee hours of the morning. The old man turned, met the
driver's gaze, and remarked simply, almost solemnly: "El Señor
Coyote." I, too, held the outline of that mammal in my vision: fur
aglow in the headlights, bushy tail dramatically pointed behind its
sleek body, head cocked backwards as if to put a spell on the bus. It
was my first animal for the new year.

Native Americans know Coyote as the multi-faced Old Man, the
Trickster, the wise fool, a four-legged magician capable of illusion and
transformation. A beast who can rise and run on two legs and use the
other two as arms like humans do. Coyote is essential to the Navajo

creation myth. He plays a lusty, always-in-trouble teacher figure in the stories of dozens of tribes indigenous to the North American continent. He reminds us that it is silly to continue on into a perfunctory existence of habitually being fooled. He does this not through rhetoric but by example. He is more often the victim of his tomfoolery. Politicians, take note!

There are books that elaborate on the habits of "Señor Coyote": Hope Ryden's *God's Dog*, Frank J. Dobie's *The Voice of the Coyote*, Barry Lopez's *Giving Birth to Thunder, Sleeping with his Daughter*—to name a few. But one needs direct experience. Firsthand sittings with Native American storytellers, repeated fireside listening to Anglo, Basque and Hispanic ranchers or sheepherders; even trappers like old man Mack Thibodeaux who's probably taken more coyotes in New Mexico than any other man alive. Yet his respect for the animal runs par with his trap record. He's a part-time consultant to university scientists and is probably more knowledgeable and respectful of the animal's tricks than most hip coyote-reverencers who pretend to know the animal but have never been licked in the face by one. Mack's got plenty of tales about coyotes that've outsmarted him in the past twenty-five years. He was the first to make me aware that the coyote who seems to be tracking young cattle for a noontime snack might be after something else. "It's not the meat, it's the calf dung the coyote's after. That hot paddy is rich with the mother's milk."

There are songwriters and poets—Joni Mitchell and Simon Ortiz, for example—who are quick to point out that you can know Coyote in a bar, near the edge of town, in redrock washes, city dumps, jails, churches or even hear them calling from tumble-down steeple tops. You can switch Coyote on and off over radio channels. Coyote calls long distance from railroad stations or granite-dome overlooks. There are arroyos, canyons, valleys, creeks and settlements all over New Mexico named Coyote. I've spent ten years on and off in one of these remote places. The locals, especially the *ancianos*, the very old, have chased after Coyote and been chased by him in return. They've named rock formations, restaurants, railroad sidings and family health clinics after Coyote and they've got plenty of stories about Coyote disguised as tax collector or enroute on some far-fetched mission as a smuggler.

Paralleling these Coyote tales are hundreds of folktales about La Llorona, the Wailing Woman, who appears at night, changing form, looking for her lost children, screaming with laughter, pity, regret, craziness. A teller of La Llorona stories sticks to his tale and makes no connections between the screams of Wailing Woman and those of four-legged creatures. But I do. A few summers back, I wrapped up for some shut-eye in my mountain cabin. The full moon was shining brightly. Shortly before dawn I woke to a series of piercing screams, each followed by a long, drawn-out gasp. Somewhere down the canyon a woman was being strangled.

I jumped into my clothes and took off for my neighbor's farmstead, but halted immediately. The full moon was red, blood red. It hung limp and dim over the western ridge, hardly casting a shadow. The screams came again. But clearly not from my neighbor's. They were high-pitched cries from my right, toward the sandstone clefts. Next morning, talking and walking with my neighbor, I found that no one was trying to strangle her; the screams were not hers. The moon had gone dim because of a total eclipse. As for the cries, I was tempted to pin them to La Llorona or Coyote, but when we explored the nearby sandstone ledges we found the impressive tracks of a mountain lion. The cat was in heat. Or, simply reacting to the darkened moon.

In New Mexico the term "Coyote" is used to designate a person who is in between, a halfbreed. A "mixed person, little of both, not quite of one world or of the other." So, the Coyote knows a lot about either side of his heritage, enough to get by securely in each world; and to get away with a hell of a lot in between. I've pondered this usage, and often I've thought of myself as a kind of Coyote, not quite secure in the world of humans, more often content to follow intuitions that connect me with nature, dream time, and the spirits that dwell in wild country that keep one on his toes with an inevitable mix of terror and awe. A Japanese poet, Takamura Kōtarō, wrote most effectively about what I mean to express:

"What is it but the slough of myself that's
mingling in the human realm?
To tell you honestly,
I belong to the family of quadrupeds that
live on a wild mountain like this.
I'm not what's called a beast
but a creature totally new."*

As a child, I called the Coyote in me the Dogwolf. This was the little beast inside me that knew what adults thought *wrong*, could just as well be *right*. By following the Dogwolf, I could track through historical time and re-establish myself with a mythical voice. The Dogwolf's energy bubbled up from the unconscious to be fueled by direct experience and quick insight as opposed to the gaining of knowledge through logical or empirically verifiable hand-me-downs. Dogwolf was a totem identification with that part of me that seemed "right" and couldn't say "no." A pet name for impulse, the personification of intuition. Like Coyote, the Dogwolf was eager to take one's philosophizing and turn it upside down. He could never hold back. He jumped up and down. A moondog. A true luna-tick. At night he restlessly nestled down to be swept away by his incessant dreaming. It's the same with Coyote. He leaps out of man's chest without control. He gives away our emotions, holding back nothing. No logic. No shame.

* From *Chieko and Other Poems of Takamura Kōtarō*, The University of Hawaii, Honolulu, 1980

The definition of Coyote as a person "not quite of one world or of the other" is applicable to shamanism, too. The scholar, Mircea Eliade, once reported a shaman in British Columbia who spoke "Coyote language" in his incantations. The shaman of Siberia and Mongolia perfected the art of flight and thus was of a singled-out cult, destined to inhabit neither the "over" nor "under" worlds, but devoted to moving between earth and sky, human and non-human worlds. The shaman was a Coyote. His "trot" was bestial, of four legs. It took him from earthy ravines to those of starry crevasses. He could explore the realm of the dead in order to help souls pass from the physical world to the ephemeral.

There is yet another type of Coyote who straddles two hemispheres but hails from neither. I speak here of the pilgrim in perpetual journey who travels not for entertainment, but to remain tuned to the vital issues of existence as lived by people outside his usual territory. Han Shan, Bashó, Issa, Ryókan—these historic Chinese and Japanese poets are examples of true wanderers; Coyotes who took to the road, gained clarity through the inevitable chaos, conflicts, and question-raising that vagabonding brought them. They experienced immense freedom but adjunct loneliness, too. They knew full well the outward journey was a symbolic one, paralleling an inward one; an exploration of the ancient and mysterious substrata buried deep in another time zone. These Coyotes were risk takers. They broke cultural rules, disregarded social barriers, walked the thin edge between myth and reality, had one foot in solitude and the other in camaraderie, and worked their ways through the enormous psychological geographies of heaven and hell.

Ultimately, all Coyote tales, all facts from wildlife experts, all trickster-tellings indigenous to our continent, do not ring true until one directly observes Coyote. I used to spend dusk in the Bosque del Apache game reserve north of Truth or Consequences, watching Coyote meander among willows and sorghum fields talking to himself, back-tracking, circling something or other with extreme curiosity. Occasionally—almost with definite interval and precise rhythm—he would turn his head and lift his tail to the four directions, calculating, inspecting, pondering to "non-think." Finally he would break into a run onto a dirt road in a hilarious *trot-hop trot hop hoppity-hop* series of antics. Then, for no apparent reason, he would hang a sharp left into the desert underbrush. His presence in my binoculars would be replaced by strata of snow geese, sandhill cranes, and musical puffs of songbirds landing in a nearby marsh to roost.

As for Old Man Coyote's trickster image—it's for real. I like to pass on a story concerning a certain lazy afternoon a friend of mine spent with some oldtimers looking out from their back porch into a series of mesas and gullies, a few rows of corn and a chicken coop in the foreground. Everybody was talking, sipping casually on beers, when a coyote danced up out of a nearby arroyo, crazily hopping through the corn, each move bringing him a little closer to the homestead. This drew silence, amazement, and a little bit of laughter from the onlookers. Coyote was really making a clown out of himself, being real silly, miming and stealing closer. But at a certain calculated instant, when Old Man Coyote had everyone rocking back on benches and chairs, he took a sidelong glance out of one eye—and lo!—made a lightning streak for the nearest hen in the chicken coop. And he was off with it before anyone had a second thought on what to do!

Soon the ethereal silence vibrates with a deep, omnipresent chanting.

RETURN TO HOPI

O f my favorite sparsely-settled arid uplifts in the world, the Hopi heartland is one. In mid-July, when the lower Chihuahua Desert becomes absolutely unbearable, it's time to head north—to Four Corners Country, to the high desert of the Colorado Plateau where Utah, Colorado, Arizona and New Mexico come together. Not that political boundaries define the region, but that their intersection serves as quick reference. In essence, Four Corners is "red geography." The presence of Native American languages—those spoken by Utes, Navajos and Hopis—is the best indicator that you are within its boundaries. So is the redrock: vermillion cliffs banded pink and cream; gray striations of fossil deposit capped by rosy sandstone; crimson hogbacks; coral dunes shifting between wildly-slanting, balanced-rock hoodoos. Everyone has a definition of which sacred mountain, trading post, or waterpocket forms the limits of Four Corners. A psychic map might well accompany the geographer's map, for this is a land where mind and mirage overlap.

The silence. The vastness.

One always experiences a reduction of stature here. You become small, humble, part of the whole. A mystic might say God began to take shape from the earth here. A geologist might wander seeking some chronological meaning to the land, only to become aimless in direction, pushed and pulled by magnetic streams, lost in a dreamscape of swirling mica and amethyst dust. Ironically, it is the fact that people live out here that makes it wild—particularly the Hopi Indians who have made the isolate mesa tops of northern Arizona their home. Who sing and dance and farm and pray and procreate in a landscape that is at once enchanting, at once imposing with its superior presence of mystery and grandeur.

Other deserts bear resemblance. Ladakh, with its moon-like crevasses tucked behind the shadow of the Himalayas, high on the Tibetan Plateau. Its dun-colored crags topped with barely-discernible *gompas*—Buddhist monasteries built of mud and stone—reminiscent of Hopi villages. Or, Bolivia. Especially the altiplano, where it drops from 20,000-foot volcanoes into the forever rainless Atacama. In all of these places—Ladakh, Hopi, Bolivia—one is lost to the vastness. No footholds. Only the dizziness of profound emotion, ears ringing from lack of oxygen. Blood thumping in erratic beats. A great star-sapphire sky above. Snow-fangs in the far distance. The zenith a spotless mirror needled with dancing electrons.

There is another similarity. The masked dances. All three geographies are inhabited by peoples whose rituals persist far back into prehistory. Animist traditions that are strongly alive in the 20th century. Not merely surviving, but enduring. Luring you into ecstatic reverie at the planet's edge. Long ago these peoples chose to remain close to heaven, at one with the clouds, guarding their prophecies, keeping their mythology alive.

Sparsity of water. Sparsity of food. Sparsity of color. A sparsity which tunes the psyche into a world of which this one is only a shadow. Life lived in a kind of transparence. Sky meeting earth. Fiery juxtapositions of light and shadow. Homes built upon rotund rim-rock which, in the last afternoon sunbeams, becomes translucent as polished amber.

• • •

It is the Hopi people, especially, that keep the world in motion—in perpetual balance—by a continuous cycle of song and dance. From the sky villages of Oraibi, Hotevilla, Bacavi, Shongopovi, Shipaulovi, Mishongnovi, Sichomovi, Hano and Walpi the sound of the dancing kachinas spreads out over the desert.

The ever-changing drone of their mesmerizing chants approximates the subtle variations of the landscape below—the colors, the geologic patterns. Sometimes the dancers hit a vocal pitch which rises into the exact shape of the topography of the desert—the anticlines, the finned islands of igneous rock, a wavering mirage, a phantom hogback. Or, the pitch breaks abruptly into faults and deep folds. One sees the incredible shapes and colors of the dancers, hears their muffled voices, then swings the eye into the immense ocean of sand hundreds of feet below—and hears the kachinas' voices repeated, echoed, magnified in that great dusty sea. Mountains lift, stone outcrops becoming pulsing chords of changing color in ethereal suspension between earth and heaven.

Concepts of space are woven together with life. The serpentine topography reoccurs in intricately-choreographed dance movements. Flashing streams, spiraling waterfalls, zigzag lightning, slithering snakes: all are richly embroidered in black and red thread on the dancers' kilts. Terraced clouds, terraced pueblos, terraced mesas: all are replicated in the shapes of wooden headboards—painted *tablitas*—

worn by male and female dancers.

The year is divided by summer and winter solstices. Rituals follow the sun. And bring the rain. Lightning flashes from a giant thunderhead and creates vertical union between heaven and earth. Rain dashes upon mesa tops and creates shelves of dancing water. Cliff edges glitter with silver fringe. Canyonsides become moving sheets of water. The eye scans the landscape, feels over the wrinkled desert far below as if it were a page of Braille. A rainbow appears. A prismed vibration of sound. The undersides of departing cumulus clouds blush with the reflection of the garnet sands below.

●　　●　　●

I am driving northwest from Window Rock, through Round Top, Shadow Springs, across the grasslands of the Navajo Reservation. Headed for the great midsummer celebration of the Hopi Niman Kachina. The going home of the kachinas—those other-worldly masked dancers personifying the invisible spirits of life. Of all the rituals in the Southwest this is perhaps the most solemn, the most melancholy. For this is the time when the Hopis gather to bid farewell to the kachinas who've been dancing and singing for the people all summer. The day has come for them to depart southwest toward their home on the far horizon—Arizona's San Francisco Peaks. Niman Kachina also celebrates fertility, the successful maturation of corn and beans so lovingly and tryingly nourished into fruition. Heat and moisture have mingled above the mesas. The season of terraced clouds has climaxed.

At Keams Canyon I stop to gas up. Plenty of Navajos doing the same. The old trading-post parking lot is filled with pickups of every size and description. Old guys wearing thick glasses, plaid shirts and big black hats piling groceries into the backs of trucks, between grandmothers in velveteens and kids in their *Hulk* and *Madonna* t-shirts.

Everyone conversing, having a good time, raising a shoulder-jerking chuckle. Eating yellow popsicles. Licking vanilla ice creams whose chocolate shells slip off in the piercing afternoon sun.

Then they are gone. A modern caravan of mud-splattered, high-wheeled trucks: gold, green, red and silver. Stalactites of caked mud hanging from bumpers. Layers of mud splashed over windshields, save for where the wipers have arced their rubber blades. The old women again, in scarves and puffy blouses and wide skirts, facing backwards in the pickup beds. Growing smaller and smaller down the highway. Mint-green velveteens. Violets. Apricots. Midnight blues. Chromes and calicos.

Vanished.

•   •   •

Second Mesa. Hopi Land. Bed down for the night under a billion stars. The Milky Way a shifting thread of luminescence, like the path of cornmeal mixed with flaked turquoise upon which the masked gods walk. Inside its glow a coyote barks. I smell dust; rain from far away; dry pungence of *Artemisia tridentada*, big sage. Next morning, rise early.

Shongopavi. Amazed to find myself here. Head pivoting to take it all in. Little details of swept-earth patios whose broom strokes resemble underwater currents or wind through rice grass. A stack of juniper wood all hairy and twisted—not chainsawed but axed—under a window whose blue frame reveals a transistor radio, antenna taped with a tinfoil square; and a kachina doll carved from cotton-wood, tubular nose painted red-orange, eyes shaped like marigolds.

At the edge of the mesa are dung piles near pottery-firing areas. Stacks of burnt rock and rusted tin. A squat flat-roofed house whose porch overlooks eternity. A garland of green chili turning red with the heat. A yarn-tied strand of blue corn against a gray-blue adobe facade. Handprints in the swirls of dried plaster. Wrinkled houses. Wrinkled faces. Wrinkled mesa tops. Cedar smoke erupting from sparking tin chimneys. Boiling food. Baking bread. Percolating coffee. Green chilies popping on cast-iron stove tops. Clatter of pans and snap of kindling wood. Everywhere, children waking from under flannel blankets on roof tops.

A bowlegged elderly woman climbing the weather-bleached rungs of a ladder to feed raw chunks of meat to a young eagle tethered to a clay chimney. Later, this same eagle will be sacrificed as part of the Niman ceremony. Its feathers will be plucked and used in future rituals to carry prayers aloft, to insure the well being of our planet. When given the meat the eagle extends its wings to guard the platter, bows its head for several minutes in meditation. Assured that no predator lurks, it finally feasts. At which point the sun rises. Lemon yellow in a mercurous sky.

I stand in silence, remembering the words of a Navajo friend: "You pray in darkness, before bed. Like they taught me in missionary school. But our customs are different. We pray outside, in the morning light. After sleep. We thank the sun for another night of safety, for blessing the new day."

I close my eyes as the first beams of sun brighten the old walls of Shongopavi. Not in imitation of my friend. Rather, it is simply an impulse. That I am here, fully, and grateful for it.

On the drive up here I saw a bumper sticker: "Honk If You'd Like To Be Indian." I smile to myself, knowing outsiders like me— *bahanas*—love to fantasize a life on these mesas. No, I am not Hopi. Yes, I am drawn back again and again. No, I could not live here. Yes, the restrictions and demands of life lived full time in these sky villages would be far too great for me to adhere to. The most honest thing I can do is admit to my status as a visitor. One who comes to look, to be assured that the values he upholds—honesty, clarity, compassion, a sense of at-one-ment with the universe—are indeed meaningful.

The clatter of shells and swish of clothing. Bells jingling, thoughts broken. The kachina are here! Up, over the mesa's golden rim and into the plaza they come—about forty Hemis ("far away") Kachinas and ten or eleven Kachina Manas (men impersonating Hopi women). The Hemis Kachinas are among the most impressive of the Hopi kachinas—wearing masks half turquoise, half yellow ochre. Narrow horizontal eye slits. Spotted cloud humps painted above the eyes. Little white circles descending down the mask centers to meet giant Douglas-fir ruffs around the dancers' necks. Huge painted headboards tiered with clouds, painted with geometric rain shafts which are simultaneously thick blue streams of moisture falling from heaven, and phallic towers of growth shooting upward, returning energy to the universe. Topping the headboards are eagle, turkey and macaw feathers, and bobbing stems of wild grass. The reverse sides of the headboards are decorated with carved and painted frogs, butterflies, squash blossoms, rainbows, pollywogs and bright clusters of maize. Sprays of iridescent parrot feathers quiver above the backs of the impersonators' heads as they nod and turn.

From the waist up the dancers are naked, bodies painted black, inscribed with interlocking crescents: symbols of outreach and clasping, of friendship and union. All of the Hemis Kachinas wear kilts, sashes, strands of yarn, turquoise jewelry, silver, jet, mother-of-pearl, coral and pumpkin shell. Arm and wrist bands are decorated with cloud, snake, and lightning abstractions. Each dancer wears leather moccasins; every right leg is strapped with a turtle-shell rattle whose inside clatters with deer hooves. An abundance of fir sprigs wave from the waist sashes and arm bands of the dancers—keeping rhythm to the beat of the stamping feet, the leg rattles, the gourd rattles held in the right hands, additional fir sprigs in the left.

It is tiring, almost, to take it all in. The eye focuses and goes dizzy, relieves itself elsewhere, then closes to the beat—the trance-evoking chant resonating from the dancers' masks; from all around their bodies. It is relaxing, for a moment, to observe the simpler attire of the Kachina Manas: whorled black wigs, feather beards, odd yellow face masks with red bangs of hair down to the eye slits. Traditional women's mantas, tall white moccasins. Each mana bears a gourd-shell resonator, a notched stick, a deerbone scraper with which to create a rasping sound while the Hemis Kachinas dance.

Two Snow Maidens appear with the manas. Solid white faces. Tubular mouths. Wigs of white cotton. Cotton neck ruffs. Suddenly the eye notices two Hoho Manas between the Snow Maidens. Solid black masks—save for the crescent designs connected with zigzagging white rain down their fronts. And, on the backs, spread-legged frogs. Animals associated with rain. Amphibians. Two-world beings which sing and jump from ponds during the fertile monsoons of the desert year.

As many times as I have witnessed this ceremony, nothing remains familiar. The eye catches an entire mask reflected in the wide, dark pupil of a child's eye. As if in a dream, one sees one's own face for a moment in the rippled glass of a little window facing the plaza. Superimposed on that face is the reflection of a dancing god. In the sky behind the god is a ruffle of blackening clouds. At once you are all—and none—of these entities. You are no longer yourself.

Perhaps the real power of the kachinas is to bring one back to a childlike innocence. To return the senses to a playful state of renewed vision. To put the self in harmony with things ephemeral as well as those within immediate grasp. It might be too simplistic to categorize the kachinas as "masked impersonators" or "living gods." Those of us who are not Hopi each have a different take on who or what the kachinas are. They function on many different, interwoven levels inside the eye of the beholder. That is their magic.

For me, the dancers are presences from a world barely remembered, still not quite accessible to the human mind. They are fragments of a divine alphabet—once commonly shared by every race and nation—come to life. They are stanzas, fiery, illuminated, of an ancient and continuing narrative. They sing rain into presence, yes. But they also sing into presence a warm, dark, fetal remembrance. They remind us of a World Before, one in which we danced with the gods; and one into which we will return if we remember to step through life with grace, courage, love, intuition—moving in harmony with the subtle, ever-present vibrations of the Creator's hand.

The Hemis Kachinas carry armloads of corn stalks and cattails tied with gifts for the children of Shongopovi. They pile them in the center of the plaza upon the sun-baked dirt. Bows, arrows, kachina dolls, piki bread, woven plaques, boxes of fruit, candies, hard-boiled eggs, cookies, toilet paper, bars of soap, pink and yellow brooms, painted wands. One by one they are plucked from the pile of brilliant green reeds and given away to the Hopi families gathered in folding chairs and on benches inside the plaza walls: grandmothers; half-blind leathery-skinned men with root-like hands; young mothers with babies shaded from the sun by colorful umbrellas; children, rocking back and forth on creaky wooden chairs; dogs, trotting in circles, checking each other out, doing the nose-sniff routine.

One becomes lost in the collective energy of the crowd. The body is simply a nerve ending, part of a giant body whose eyes and ears and throats are magic vents to a subconscious awareness shared by all. The head turns away for awhile, then turns back—and discovers that the pile of corn stalks and cattails in the plaza's center is now gone. The Hemis Kachinas have effectively distributed the reeds to the crowd. The plaza has been transformed into a living garden, everyone holding a green upright stalk, a tree, a gift. Fruit and dolls and bread and painted wooden toys are in the hands of old and young alike. Everyone's lap is overflowing with food. The miracle of the loaves and fish. Delight in the sudden multiplication of numbers!

Soon the ethereal silence vibrates with a deep, omnipresent chanting. The singer-dancers are backed only by the cerulean blue sky. Nowhere else on the North American continent does one come so close to the idea of immortality in the real world. To the right and left the Hemis Kachinas' bodies sway, turning—and turning again— in precise choreography. Lifting and setting their feet down, shaking hand rattles, rattling the deer hooves inside the turtle shells fastened to the calves. They are directed by two priests, rather plainly attired, who call out subtle shifts in position, sprinkle corn meal upon the dancers' shoulders, give orders to the Kachina Manas to bend to the ground in their corn-grinding positions. Then, in perfect unison— facing the long sinuous line of Hemis dancers—the manas scrape their deer scapulae against the notched sticks resting on their gourd resonators.

Up and down, up and down—the feet with jingling bells. In great arcs, the arms with their rattles, back and forth, back and forth—the deer bones rasping the notched painted sticks. And from everywhere around the bodies of the Hemis Kachinas resounds a deep and tremulous vibration in the morning light. A soft rhythm from hands, legs, chest, masks—breaking upon the observers in a continuous wave—heightened by the resonating quality of the plaza walls. A great sound box in which the intoned chant gently rolls and repeats itself with a slightly-out-of-synch echo, mesmerizing the onlookers.

You don't have to do anything but be. Hopi does it all to you.

As the first round of dancing progresses, I notice all sorts of people slowly moving across the flat rooftops of homes surrounding the plaza, toward the northeast. There, into a large courtyard, the risen sun casts slanting light through a hand-adzed ladder protruding from a kiva's smoke hole. When the kachinas complete their song, the Kachina Father and his assistants lead them toward that light.

Then another round of dancing in the spacious sunlit courtyard. Now the blessing of kachinas with corn meal, sprinkles of water, and a smoking pipe. Solemn and touching, and not to be repeated until the last dance of the day.

Twelve hours of nearly uninterrupted song and dance, the undulating rhythm, the chant! The village packing with people, the sun burning through kaleidoscoping clouds, the elders inside the kiva praying.

Finally—after sunset—the rhythm stops.

The Kachina Father recites his lengthy prayer and bids farewell to the Hemis Kachinas, the Snow Maidens, the Kachina Manas, the Hoho Manas. A very noble farewell, indeed. For the Hopis, young and old alike, strengthened by the presence of the dancers now have confidence to ask the gods for a few favors: that they continue to watch over the people from their sacred retreat; that they bring seeds of moisture through the dark winter months; that all growing things—plants and humans alike—be revitalized with purity and renewal.

Acknowledging the prayer of the Kachina Father and the petitioning Hopis, the leader of the Hemis Kachinas shakes his rattle. The onlookers walk lithely toward the line of masked impersonators—removing fir sprigs from their arms and waists. Planting these sprigs in the fields is to plant the entire spirit and power of a tree, is to bring to life the seeds of corn and beans in abundant germination the following year.

Now the kachinas depart. A saddening sight for the visitor. But no gesture of mourning from the Hopis. Many of them have left the rooftops before the kachinas have disappeared below Shongopovi's rim. No room to be sentimental. Only room for the ongoing rite of purification and beautification in the world of mortals.

•　　•　　•

Again, to sleep.

Under billions of stars turned inside out—every pinpoint of light vibrating with the song of the kachinas, the steps of their dance—I think to myself: today I was in a place where my heart beat rhythmically, my eyes opened wide as if they'd never experienced the world before, my flesh took wing. That is what Hopi allows us. The essence of transport. The remarkable discovery that we are but a mirror within a mirror, a song of multiplicity in which the gods exchange places with humans. And humans, like them, do a dance where body steps beyond itself and becomes spirit.

The clock hands of time turned to liquid, running into the badlands and off into an enormous gulch.

THE IDOLATER OF LOCO HILLS

Some places in Espejo County are like a great ceramic plate fashioned by a mad potter. The kiln-baked surface is glazed with lavenders, green, pewter. Into this sun-fired plateau are scratched a random network of gullies which expose an under-strata of bone and raw tendon. Mountains rim the edges of this great clay platter, but they recede from your vision as soon as you spot them. Like sunburnt drunks, they wobble, topple halfway down, then defy the gods of gravity by freezing in midair. Buttes, crags, pinnacles—they remain comically aslant, rendering the Tower of Pisa straight as a skyscraper in comparison. Here and there, it seems as if the mad potter's plan for a reasonably perfect work has been sabotaged by air bubbles, forming irreparable abysses in the surface of the giant platter. For the cowpuncher, this maze of crags and fissures is likened to a section of hell. Cows don't get sick and rustling is almost unheard of—yet cows constantly disappear.

"They just git tired a tryin' t'stand up straight alla time. An when that happins, hell—they just lose their legs and—*loop*—it's down the barrel they go, off a cliff into a canyon. Meat for the coyotes. Ain't a level place around—it's all up 'n down."

There's another reason why cattle disappear, too. Last week's *Current-Argus* headlines read:

UFO'S LINKED TO COW MUTILATIONS

Underneath, a news article revealed the strange case of a yearling heifer found near Fade-away Mountain, linking its death not to "cryptic earthbound cults" but to outer-space visitors. Police discovered scorched grass near the cow's body. The article went on:

> "Mysterious suction-cup tracks, each with a spot of oil in the center, were found leading up from the carcass to the landing site. Missing from the dead animal were the left ear, lips, heart, eyeballs, tail and anal passage—each neatly removed with surgical precision which a veteran butcher at the scene said he couldn't have duplicated. There was no blood, no indication of shooting. Radiation tests showed high radioactive counts near the carcass. State Police believe whoever—or whatever—was responsible for the mutilation arrived and departed in an airborn vehicle which left triangular depressions, about six feet apart, in the scorched area near the dead animal."

Believable or not, the Espejo County badlands are a fitting place for a space craft to set down. I am always reminded of a Salvador Dalí painting—a bit of moon-like earth scattered with melted glass and steel artifacts. A radio tower, a defense radar blinking in the sun, a heat-warped frame-and-stucco home built by a tough breed of ranchers. A cluster of squat, earthen farm buildings erected by the first Hispanic settlers. And behind it all—a watch, that dripping pocket watch. The clock hands of time turned to liquid, running into the badlands and off into an enormous gulch, a fissure which knows no bottom.

You can't trust your senses in Espejo County. There's nothing to attach your reason to. In this land you may easily mistake soft clusters of dung and marl for homes of men. Often, upon closer inspection, what you think to be homes of men turn out to be outcroppings of desert-varnished stone. Gravel roads lose their bearings, afraid to confide in the lay of the land. They stop dead just a little beyond a desert sheep camp, a drilling exploration, an abandoned prospect. Dirt paths take off from there, but not for long. Soon they run into a crag, a gorge, a river channel which has defiantly sliced through the plateau's pock-marked surface—exposing secret arrowpoints, marine skeletons, dinosaur feet, and certain fossils which still aren't completely dead. Broken autos, bathroom atomizers, polyurethane shards from picnic cups. Beer cans, synthetic baby diapers, runover dogs. Dumped two days or two thousand years ago? There is no way of telling. For decay is almost unknown here. Humidity practically nonexistent.

"They don't bury people here. They just set 'em out t'dry." That's what a cowboy on the Ajax Ranch told me.

Severe, sober, no unnecessary adornment, no superfluous adjectives to embellish the landscape. The desert forces you to read between the lines. Its tenderness is revealed only when you bend upon your knees prostrating yourself to the centipedes. And you can't look upward for long. The sky is too immense, too radiant. Words are precious. Language must be economical. The heat dries your tongue each time you open your mouth to speak. Pure ether, no density to the air. If you leave a box of matches out, it'll explode. Clouds might gather occasionally in the summer, but their pluvial drapery rarely touches the ground. You get the point of just how precious water is when you see a desert farmer wash his dinner plates in a pan of water, then bathe his feet in the same water and carry it out for his corn. Not a drop is wasted. He pours it into empty tuna cans at the base of each corn shoot, and the water leaks slowly out through a tiny nail puncture at the can's bottom. It's a daily routine. Or better, it's done in the darkness before bed, when the evaporation rate is minimal.

But the desert is an eloquent country, too. A wildflower perfumes the air one year, then disappears for another quarter-century before conditions are right for it to bloom again. Spring arrives leaf by leaf, petal by petal. Odors journey through the atmosphere singularly, like musical notes with plenty of space between each bar. They carry themselves deep into the olfactory nerves, reaching climax in the anterior of the cerebrum. A crushed sprig of sage. The rank, nostril-biting smell of a trailing buffalo gourd. Ambrosial presence of a datura blossom opening in the twilight. The musky odor of a packrat's nest under a shelf of primrose. A resinous cluster of creosote plants. The sudden, shifting waft of carrion rotting on hot tarmac.

In Espejo County one finds no Wordsworthian field to saturate the mind with an orgy of smells. Nothing rushed or flooded. A scent is here, then gone. Hours, days later, another follows. Cool, wind-sweet. Heated, nauseous. Redolent or rank. Desolation kicks the senses into new dimensions. The eyes are forced inside themselves. The brain retreats into unweighted silence. Aridity's power! Nothing to distract. Everything in the head. A shaman can lose his mind here. See through himself in the translucency. Live out his fantasies, or go crazy.

•   •   •

Sometimes, in this dehydrated expanse, my mind wanders back to a warped macadam road, narrow and sand-gutted, that leads out to that sunburnt, emerald-eyed man on the front porch of his store near what used to be Loco Hills. He was known all over Espejo County. The women of church groups used to make weekly runs to try and convert him—to save him from his "evil" ways. Perhaps it was those same church-going ladies who put the nickname on old Fred Adeline—"the Idolater of Loco Hills." It could also be that the women went out to see Fred in order to secretly seduce him, for his little clay figurines starkly represented their innermost, defiant and erotic desires. And Fred himself was a rather handsomely erotic oldtimer with a continuous bulge in his crotch. He was in his late sixties, with a full head of white hair, as strong as a horse, and he knew by heart all the Bible stories better than any professional Espejo County preacher.

"They call me an idolater, but I'm a maker. I'm so busy creatin' that I ain't got time to worship."

Fred's little gas pump and store is all that is left of the settlement of Loco Hills. The new town is located somewhere else. The store is fashioned from weather-beaten lumber, chinked with clay and covered with flattened oil cans. A scrubby tamarisk grows over the roof. Its pink and green branches are crowned with a Star-of-David radio antenna, which pulls in more static than music. In the store there's only a can of Del Monte hominy, a couple dusty containers of Spam, three or four mouse traps packaged in brittle cellophane, a kerosene-lamp chimney and an ancient tobacco advertisement depicting a young man wreathed with smoke, dressed in a prim brown suit. Under the wreath of smoke, a slogan:

SPEND THE REST OF YOUR DAYS ON VELVET

Fred's on his porch, as usual, putting the finishing touches on a small figurine of Eve, a snake coiled around her middle—which he lifts on and off, laughing. "The snake's to cover her private parts. But the snake comes up, like this . . . so's I'm not completely robbed of her beauty. Purty spicy, huh?" We walk to the rear of the store. Under the Star-of-David tamarisk he proudly takes me around his collection of handmade statuettes that would shake a nonbeliever's heart with apocalyptic revelation.

Fred hands me a pair of army binoculars and demands that I view his creations "with the power of the concentrated eye . . . up close. Go on, make 'em big. Bring 'em to life!" I fix the glasses on Moses, raised above a congregation of queens and devils and ceramic saints, on a huge pedestal of wood, epoxied with a dozen or so salvaged bicycle reflectors. "Ol' Moses gonna need a new coat of paint soon. Durn acrylics fade away in the sun, but that's no matter. When they fade, I got somethin' t'do it again. I can talk to Moses, paint his beard, retouch the numbers on his tablets. Like havin' a friend, y'know."

Across the patio is a grotto made of automobile tires, painted white, stacked around a series of posts. In the grotto is a manger filled with radio wire and a baby-doll Christ child. But Christ, instead of having a child's face, wears the head of President Kennedy. Mary and Joseph are there too. Mary with a Barbie Doll face and a healthy set of molded breasts. Joseph with a playful smile under his cloth beard. Slightly behind him a donkey brays with a black prophet on his hump.

"That's supposed t'be Martin Luther King. See, this is a political piece. Like updatin' the Bible, I figure. But no one really recognizes it as King. Just a wise man. I'm no good at look-alikes. Never learned nothin' about portrits. My friends say they can't tell the Lord from Mary Magdalene. But who cares. I'm having fun. I'm havin' somethin' to do."

Once, on a windy, dust-biting day, Fred revealed his most secret piece to me. He crouched over a canvas tarp. He untied a string. Carefully, he unwrapped a life-size plaster statue. And spoke in a serious tone. "This is somethin' I made because I jus' can't tell it in words. I'm workin' on it still. Everyone that's seen it tells me it's blamsphemy-ous. But you're young, you'll understand. They're jus' used t'thinkin' of God way up in the sky and the devil somewhere down below. But I've made 'em differently, y'see?"

God, with his hefty shoulders and flowing beard, resembled a Grecian brute. But below his shoulders I was in for a shock. The muscular plaster-of-Paris sculpture turned into a beautiful nymph with glossy breasts and exaggerated hips, a gentle mound in between. A baby (another one of Fred's plastic doll additions) nestled below one of the breasts. The figure ended in a fishtail, painted metallic blue. Fred made a grunting noise and peeled more of the plastic wrapping from the backside of the statue.

"Okay, walk around. Take a peek."

Carved into the backside of God was the devil. A Medusa-headed devil with the body of a hefty man. The devil held out a hubcap from a '53 Chevy which Fred had meticulously painted with the world. The figure's bottom half extended in the same fishtail as its other side, of course—except that the tail was spray-painted a metallic red instead of blue.

"This is my philly-sophical piece. Y'can't expect t'understand it. God. Devil. Man. Woman. Youth. Old age. Fish. Mammal. World. 'S all th' same far as I'm concerned. Why make a buncha separate pieces. 'S more fun puttin' it all t'gether way things really are. They say we was made in an image of th' Lord so I figgure th' Lord musta had good an' bad in him just like us. An' I been thinkin'—why's God hafta be justa man since it takes man *an* woman t'make a third. That' why I combined 'em. Do y'see?

.   .   .

Yes, I saw. And will always see old emerald-eyed Fred there in that biting dust of Loco Hills, the "idolater" as they called him. He's not alive anymore and they didn't bother to put his sculptures in a museum. His stuff was just carted off here and there by vandals and tourists and antique dealers. And the rest, God and the devil and the big pieces, why they were taken to the Fade-Away Mountain dump and broken to bits by the single lowering of a Cat blade. The store's a ghost now, as it almost was then. The gas pump whistles in the wind. But the Star of David is still in that Tamarisk. And there are splatters of faded paint on the cement pad near the fallen-in grotto where old Fred Adeline's creations once stood.

"They all told me I was off my rocker t'make a home here, that I'd last six weeks, if that. But the more folks told me I couldn't, the more power I got t'go ahead with it. Sometimes a man's gotta have a little barrier t'work against. A little open space t'make the right way come clear. What's good for one ain't necessarily good for another. I'm a maker, and a maker's gotta find out for himself. I don't care t'waste my time makin' my shoes fit somebody else's feet who's got a different sole than me."

That's what Fred Adeline was saying to me the last time I saw him alive. That's what made me think a guy like Fred can never really die.

Standing in front of the altar, I became part of its iconography.

MARIA ANGELA'S
MIRACULOUS TORTILLA

The first time I drove into the town of Lake Arthur, New Mexico, it was a drab Sunday morning, late November 1977. Little cyclones of dust swirled along the curbs of the one-and-only main drag. Barren willows stood out in the distance. A half-dozen people hunkered along the running boards of dented pickups in front of Maria Angela's modest green stucco home. A family dressed in black and white conversed in Spanish, waiting outside her door for the small living room to clear. They, like so many others—locals and outsiders—had come for a first hand look at Christ's apparition on a thick, white-flour tortilla, the kind traditional to native New Mexican cookery. It was Mrs. Angela's tortilla. She had saved the portion on which the face appeared, framed it under glass and placed it on a coffee-table altar with two candles, a vase of fresh flowers and a crucifix.

I waited along with the other families, signed a finger-stained register and moved up to the altar. The portion of the tortilla that had been preserved was toasted in only one place, and that burnt mark—from the kitchen skillet—had produced an extraordinary likeness of Jesus Christ wearing a crown of thorns. It was a portrait in miniature, comparable to a Leonardo da Vinci ink drawing. The Prophet's sepia-tone eyes sparkled with pinpoints of topaz light as they stared at me. Slowly, that light moved toward the outer fringes of Christ's head, until a halo was formed. It was the second time in my life that I'd witnessed an aura around a subject's head—not just imagined it.

The first incident was ten years previous, in Ecuador, where I saw an orange corona around the head of a peasant's dog. José María Mendieta and I were sitting under the subtropic sun, our bodies shaded by his thatched-roof porch. We were casually meditating on the dog—discussing labor laws, Sputnik, Caryl Chesman and Catholicism—when the dog's head suddenly lit up. I remember José turning to me, saying: "Well, what have we here? A little miracle, eh—not in heaven but directly in front of our eyes. See! This is how it happens if you just have your eyes open all the time."

When the crowd in Maria Angela's living room cleared, I spoke with her. She was a middle-aged, hazel-complected, soft-featured woman. As she talked, a warmth spread about her that could not simply be pinpointed to her calm brown eyes or smile. Her beauty was everywhere in the room. This is what she had to say:

"I had prepared a sack of tortillas and brought them to the table to roll a burrito for my husband. I laid one tortilla out flat, put the beans in, folded it once, twice, and on the third fold I suddenly saw Jesus. Right there! My family saw him, and my neighbors. Word got around. Even as far as Albuquerque people were talking. The archbishop read about us in the newspapers. He claimed the incident was a matter of coincidence and warned me to keep things quiet. But how do you keep something like this secret? It is a good sign. We would like to build a chapel around it. Father Finnigan, at the church here, blessed the tortilla. Everyone has come to see it. The miracle has kept my family together. It has brought many good strangers into my home. My husband has quit drinking. And I have started to dream again. What is there to hide?"

. . .

A couple of months later I again visited Mrs. Angela. It was a drizzly winter weekday—the smells of sheep manure and oil refineries saturated the hazy blue air. Maria's house stood looking like most other Main Street homes, save that her living room had been partitioned from the rest of the house and made into a chapel. A separate door entering from the sidewalk was about to be installed. "We will keep it open twenty-four hours a day," Mrs. Angela told me.

I entered the shrine, and all objects, every detail at once, flooded my sight as if through a pinhole camera with a tremendous depth of field. The little register book had gone from 2,000 entries to 8,000. A large velvet painting of Christ, once behind the altar, now hung on a separate wall. In its place was a large portrait of the mysterious Lady of Guadalupe—who some believe to be the Conquistador's replacement for the Aztec's all-mother goddess, Tonantzín. Above the Lady was the Mexican flag. Below, a lithograph of St. Michael killing a dragon. And below that, the tortilla—now in a handmade case with a glass cover held down by screws.

Standing in front of the altar I became part of its iconography. I remained silent until Mrs. Angela appeared in her bedroom slippers and our eyes met. "Do you see it differently now?" she asked. "Some people return and tell me the image is changing, that the hair and beard are growing." I replied that the image held the same shape and radiance as when I first saw it. The idea of the hair and beard growing reminded me of a statue of Christ in a church on the Mexican border. Mrs. Angela smiled. "I know of that Christ. He's in Ojinaga. Some say his toenails are growing. And when it is time to change his garments, it is such a struggle that it takes three or four people to do it."

As we conversed, the sparkle of miniature silver figurines filled my eyes: hearts, hands, eyes, cows, human torsos—all pinned above the altar, dangling from pink ribbons. One of these little "milagros" was a primitively-cast profile of a man's body left by someone who had come to pray before the tortilla. Mrs. Angela said a man who had cancer in the cheek was seeking a cure. I examined the dye-cast image and thought of an incident that happened some years back, in Holman village, northern New Mexico. The famous "Wall of Holman."

On the white-washed side of an adobe schoolhouse, under the night brightness of a street lamp, appeared Christ's face. When word of that "miracle" spread, thousands flocked to the scene. People from as far as Ohio, Florida, Mexico City and Cheyenne. One man shot at the image, some laughed, others saw nothing at all. Many people were seeking an answer to their prayers, or a reaffirmation of their belief in God. A few eager Holman residents took advantage of the apparition and set up taco stands, sold pop and even souvenir postcards and fluorescent bumper stickers which read: "I Have Seen The Wall."

Day by day strange prayer-offerings were deposited on a table in front of the miraculous wall. A cutout photo of a sick relative wedged into a glass candle holder. A silver eye. A tiny wooden leg tied to a miniature aluminum crutch with a pink ribbon. A scribbled prayer stuffed into an old shoe—an incredible shoe—fashioned to fit a deformed foot, with openings cut into the leather for bunions and corns. A pair of thick eyeglasses accompanied by a note: "Please help my cataracts." A broken wallet with a bouquet of wilted violets and a letter: "Please make Teodoro pay me the money he owes." And several other objects, plastic rosaries and personal requests, one of which read: "I would like for people to like me."

The media picked up on the phenomenon. The archbishop refused to sanction the apparition. He claimed that there was nothing to see and discouraged people from worshiping the wall. Eventually the wall was repainted and had a new bulb placed in the street lamp. But the miracle continued to happen, despite skeptics who claimed that residents of Holman were being hoaxed and were seeing nothing more than an "effect" or optical illusion. Yet I remember throngs of people standing there together bound tightly by that effect. For once men weren't getting drunk in bars and women weren't slaving in kitchens. Everyone was in Holman, the children, too—having a good time, content to be blessed by the apparition, without having to prove or disprove its authenticity. Likewise Maria Angela pointed out that her tortilla caused strangers to "come close, in a town in the middle of nowhere."

To be able to wonder together at the incomprehensible is a vital experience. The energy behind this awe depends upon an alchemy and a mystique which defies traditional science. New Mexico's Hispanic elders, in particular, retain a humbleness which allows receptivity to the marvelous, the extraordinary. They are content to live for today while others struggle ahead for tomorrow. I am reminded again of the Ecuadorian peasant, José María Mendieta, who in his conversation about miracles and the aura around the dog's head, implied that the metaphysical readily makes itself available in the world around us, "if you just have your eyes open."

Our world "miracle" comes from the Latin *mirari* which means "to wonder." *Mirari* in turn, finds its roots in the Sanskrit *smayate*: "he smiles." Which takes me back to Mrs. Maria Angela at Lake Arthur. Her gentle outward generosity. Her unhesitating smile. And those words of hers: "What is there to hide?"

The labyrinthine voice below swoons me into its rhythm . . .

THE DESERT AS MIRROR

The desert has to call you into it. You cannot easily make it your own. Some sort of signal must be given. I've come here because the landscape matches an interior one, something dreamed, a place very alive. Whether I shut my eyes or contemplate with them open, the same scenery is there—a perfect match. The desert is a mirror, the physical replica of my unconscious self. In the clarity of its air, under the sharpness of its skies, within the dance of heatwaves and ghost imagery of a mirage, the mind stops turning, the body becomes still, unnecessary baggage evaporates. With lightness, the eye takes hold.

As a young boy I first crossed the Mohave with my father at the wheel of his turtle-shaped 1947 Hudson—listening to his tarantula tales, traveling over Arizona's cinder-red roads, watching mountains move forward through the windshield, rain shafts playing tricks with volcanic hills. In a little leatherbound notebook I recorded names: Kaibab, Meteor Crater, Jackrabbit, Yellowhorse, Iyanbito, Laguna,

Albuquerque. The desert swept upward, into the high Chihuahuan mesas, and met with a horizon of marching thunderheads, bolts of lightning; a wet, stimulating turbulence.

Later, when I was ten, I flew the same route by airplane: a TWA triple-tailed Constellation. While my mother nervously prayed her rosary I moved from one side of the fuselage to the other, peering from the little portholes that served to frame the world in glassy mandalas. There was Meteor Crater, its curled ochre lip ablaze with a wreath of golden light; there was the Grand Canyon, shadowed like a tapestry, vermillion and purple; and now—the buttes and tumbled mountains of New Mexico; the mint greens and rosy flourescence of its painted desert.

As a grown man I've recrossed my childhood trail several times. In the desert I begin to grasp a part of me that hides itself in other environs. There is something of my personality in the shape and color of the land, in the brilliant, quiet light of solitude, in the sharpness of edge meeting edge, sky cutting apart earth. The desert speaks with the ideal language of a poem: emotionally charged, alive with surprise and mystery, a topography bathed in light, christened with sudden shadows, full of passionate syllables—landforms—rising and falling with little predictability.

In places like Ashislepah, Abiquiu, Canyon de Chelly and Monument Valley, the high desert resembles the crazy isobar features that I squiggled as a child at my drawing table, listening to Beethoven or The Lone Ranger; using thick, black Dixon Beginner's pencils on newsprint to draw shapely continents exhibiting every imaginable climate and geography. I was the master cartographer for worlds unknown to every explorer but me. My language was the line, and the line was ceremonial: a thread extending from brain through body onto the page; a singular alphabet that spoke in one, long, silent passage—procreating as it went, bestowing dimension to the flat surface over which it rolled, a sonorous filament intimate with the pronouncement of my dreams.

Recently, I came across a wonderful book* by the poet John Haines wherein he describes the "dream journey" and "actual life," telling us that "the two seem to touch now and then, and perhaps when men lived less complicated lives the two were not separate at all, but continually one thing." He mentions a Mohave Desert tribe, the Yuma Indians, who "dreamed at will, and moved without effort from waking into dreaming. Life and dream were bound together, and in this . . . a kind of radiance, a very old and deep assurance that life has continuity and meaning, that things are somehow in place. It is the journey resolved into one endless present."

This "endless present" described clearly those childhood travels with my parents, into Sierra Nevada mountain meadows, along California's Big Sur Coast, across the desolate surface of the Mohave, over the Colorado River and into the American Southwest. To travel into a place unfamiliar—then to sleep there and to witness the continuance of that new landscape inside me under the stars or in a cabin lit by the dancing flicker of kerosene lamps—was to experience time without its usual frame, was to become like a stone in a river with the world flowing endlessly around me.

Haines tells a story about a place along the Southern California coast called Pool Rock, where the Chumash Indians partook in magic rites. "We came to the rock in mid-afternoon, a great sandstone pile rising out of the foothills like a sanctuary or shrine to which one comes yearly on a pilgrimage. There are places that take on symbolic value to an individual or tribe, 'soul-resting places,' a friend of mine has called them. Pool Rock has bcome that to me, symbolic of that hidden, original life we have done so much to destroy."

The Southwestern deserts are enchanted with many such "soul-resting places." Simultaneously they are "listening places" or "story

*Living Off the Country, The University of Michigan Press, Ann Arbor, 1981.

spots." Spider Rock, Atlatl Rock, the confluence of the Big and Little Colorado Rivers, Enchanted Mesa, and a giant neck of hardened lava which the Navajos call "Tsé Bit'áí" immediately come to mind. The latter formation, known as "Shiprock" by some, thrusts 1500 feet above a bleak, mile-high plateau near Four Corners. On first glance, and because mapmakers have conditioned us to the image, we do see a ship. But look again and the rock does not resemble a ship at all. Instead, it is exactly what the Navajos believe it to be: the ragged tail plumes of a giant bird that plummeted headfirst into the sagebrush, leaving only its rear feather sticking up as a reminder of the mythical realm from which it descended.

The old storytellers find it comprehensible to measure time in concentric circles, or in terms of the space between the rungs of the imagination's ladder. They have an amusing time with a geologist's verification that "the rock is magma, its age about 3,000,000 years." For the storyteller or shaman, time and space are one and inter-changeable, myth and reality are not separate entities, and the world of apparent opposites—light and shadow, male and female, birth and death—are the only temporary dualities pointing toward an ultimate Mystery, a force beyond pairs of opposites.

Just east of my home along the Rio Grande north of Albuquerque are the Sandia Mountains. They rise as a single, craggy block of billion year-old granite capped with 300,000,000 year-old sedimentary rock. At the base of these mountains one might find pottery shards 500 years old; higher up, a spearhead 10,000 years old; and still higher, a fossil clam or trilobite dating 250,000,000 years. From the topmost ridge, facing northwest, the cliffs fall steeply toward the greenery hugging the Rio Grande—the cottonwood, willows, tamarisk and Rusian olives—and the quietly camoflaged pueblos of San Felipe, Sandia, Cochiti, Zia, Santa Ana and Santo Domingo.

Sitting between these cloud-swooped crags, I've often felt that someone down in one of those villages must be simultaneously looking up at me—a person indigenous to this land. Perhaps a grandfather with his grandson, recalling a story more primordial than any of the earth history I have mentioned. Or perhaps a singer, able to move the mountain with his song, or lift himself into the highest pinnacles with each rise of his voice, each prance of the foot.

What I am getting at is concisely stated in another passage by John Haines: "When life is simplified, its essence becomes clearer, and we know our lives as part of some ancient human activity in a time measured not by clocks and calendars but by the turning of a great wheel, the positions of which are not wage hours, nor days and weeks, but immense stations called Spring, Summer, Autumn, and Winter."

A friend of mine once remarked that "home is where you carry it, portable like the heart." But home is also where the body locates itself, like a seed within the landscape, like a sperm magnetized by an egg— lodging itself in a place where dream reality and physical reality perfectly converge. The great scholar of mythology, Joseph Campbell, once remarked: "The Holy Land is no special place. It is every place that has ever been recognized and mythologized by any people as home."

It is the spirit of the land, the empty horizon, the abrupt geologic changes, the drama of clouds, the honored power spots, the ongoing Native American ritual-drama in praise of earth as mother and begetter that both keeps me on edge and makes me at home in the Southwest. It is also the presence of landscape as metaphor: that we live in and wander through geography that beckons the imagination with symbols for another reality.

The desert is a mirror reflecting those solitary places inside us where we occasionally permit ourselves to be overwhelmed by emptiness, to receive the blessing of silence under the sky's immensity in order to regain foothold, clarity, a sense of our place in the universe. The jagged mountain ranges with their sweeping, purple alluvial aprons represent barriers inside us, hidden with passes that we must find to cross on through. The little oases that suddenly show their grassy blades and break the assault of heat replicate places of pause and renewal in an interior journey, as well as those of life's greater pilgrimage from infancy through old age.

Geography, in a sense, begins within, erupts from the imagination, becomes real as we walk, disappears as we turn our heads backwards, and continues to be remembered as strange, telegraphic teletype spelling out metaphors for a world beyond the one we physically occupy. I am taken back to the idea of "endless present," to the merge and continuous harmony of waking and dreaming, to the metaphor of the masked kachinas dancing in a sinuous line in the summer plazas at Hopi: the kachinas personifying Nature; its original, unbroken rhythm; a river of song shrouded by huge thunderheads darting lightning. The pure state of Nature, before it was interrupted by humans.

The desert is a bright mirror, a sea without water. When I look into it I see the face of an old man, a bit of the child, a strong presence of the mythic, an open textbook of evolution. It is living topography, full of signs, alive with stories that can be read with the feet as well as with the eye. Each waterhole, every sphinx-like formation bears the touch of someone greater than us whose deeds run far back into another time. The hummingbird, the yellowjacket, the coyote, the raven, the lizard—they too are carry-overs from another time—when humans and animals spoke the same language, performed the same tasks, mingled together and knew harmony.

I stand in one spot, and the compass begins to spin. I begin to walk, and trails don't lead anywhere. When I stop, they stop. There is no tense. I am here and there at once. I am big, I am small. The mesas, their weathered bodies suddenly broken by labyrinthine folds of river-cut rock, are exact replicas of my childhood drawings. It is as if those sheets of newsprint, those marks of graphite, had suddenly become three-dimensional, taken on proportion, overwhelmed the eye. Now, as a grown man, I walk into them, delighted to reacquaint myself with their scale and rhythm, their color and transparency. As an artist I am engulfed by my own line.

There is one such "drawing-come-to-life" place in southern Utah that calls me back often. Downward I trek, leaving the slickrock mesas as if leaving a plane of consciousness for an interior, subconcious depth. A series of prehistoric footholds safely brings the feet to a weave of sandy, canyon-bottom passages. There, with towering arches surrounding, I brush pink sand from shins and palms and reflect on the downward journey. A passage not simply *through* geologic time, but *of* mythic time. The temporal world of everyday doings above. The world of shadows, an eternal place of wonder below.

In the process of walking I have somehow managed to lose my own shadow. It was alongside for awhile, then wandered off by itself and evaporated. Released from that shadow, I am forced to be content without it, to be my own company, at solace with the world. Like those that have gone before me, I am awed by the world that surrounds. The human body has slipped into the greater body of the planet. Here, one resides inside and outside the flesh simultaneously. The word "transcendental" is no longer an abstract experience.

Around me, the bright stone ascends dramatically upward, contrasting its redness with the sky, optically creating a black zenith inside the retina. In this blackness two ravens suddenly become silver. They dip and caw and freefall, wheeling like mirrored spokes as they pass from view. Below me, cupped into the smooth, ochre sandstone, is a *tinaja*—a bowl-like depression where rainwater has collected. Into this mirror I stare, watching my face distort and expand as water spiders dance across the surface. A pollywog moves to the center of my eyes and dives. Now, over my mouth two dragonflies hover, lovemaking in midair, their delicate, see-through

125

bodies joined in a perfect heart shape. Then, into the mirror I reach. At the *tinaja's* bottom I pluck a smooth agate and place it upon my tongue. A communion, so to speak—an act of purifying the body by asking Nature into it.

The wind picks up, slipping through rock hollows and fluted chambers with a sound like hundreds of panpipes blowing in unison. A lizard appears on a stone, a smile on its face and a very inquisitive look. It is so stationary, so very still—like an old Zen master planted there for eternity. But just as the mind speaks the word "eternity" the eye looks away for a second and when it returns the lizard has vanished.

At length, when I am ready to pick my way out of the maze, I soon discover that—though I've marked a path well with tiny cairns—the way out doesn't seem to resemble the way in. Or maybe it just looks different trekking the opposite way. For there are nooks and clefts I haven't noticed before—stone foundations, remains of miniature villages, Anasazi sites, clinging like swallows' nests to the canyon sides.

Under smooth stone overhangs, in natural amphitheaters, I find the debris of householders: painted pottery, turquoise beads, fragments of yucca-fiber sandals. There is a kiva with its roof still intact, perfect handprints in gray mud plaster. A few painted dots and spirals, serpentine lines of ochre, a row of corn stalks leafing skyward. People ate and slept here, planted food, held their ceremonies, had babies and moved on.

Suddenly, in this place of past and present merged, I remember my way. The upward ascent from dark to light is to experience a birthing— out of the earth rather than onto it, as some sort of master race. It is a humbling experience, reconfirming in that it provides a clue to how the Anasazi lived and organized themselves: with repsect to the consciousness of the planet. Earth as mother, as a living organism.

Reaching the rim where I originally descended, I pause.

This lip of smooth stone is a threshold between light and dark, inner and outer, eternal and temporal worlds. Bathed in the desert's brilliant glow, silence overwhelms the body. The labyrinthine voice below swoons me into its rhythm, releases me into the faraway scent of an afternoon thunderstorm, returns me in a whirling wind of blue dust and mica.

The landscape is made portable as its spirit enters the flesh, becomes humanized, finds dwelling, sings out again through the mouth. Each sprinkle of moisture that drifts from sky gives birth to a seed, a flower that springs upward to blossom and pollinate the stars whose carbon forms the universe, makes dandelions yellow, makes meat red.

Dusk now, disappearing light.

Between the crests of two soaring cumulus clouds, a planet appears. Darkness spreads through the desert atmosphere. Wave after wave of indigo. Distant roll of thunder. Shafts of moonlit rain. Odor of wet sage. Below me, the dream maze. Above me, the dream maze. Between, a mirror of glistening sand and tilted mesas. Everywhere, the continent is dark, laced with shadows, webbed with planet light, woven with intricate meanderings of phosphorescing reefs, underwater cities, human arteries, sea anemone, snowflakes, the roseate windows of a cathedral, the calligraphic floorplan of a mosque. Every shape and idea that humans have credited themselves with is here in the master plan of Nature. I breathe deeply of this sweet, primordial desert night and raise my arms, fingers extended, to embrace this wild and starry sky, these anonymous, flaring constellations, these blinking spirits of the departed spilling atom by atom back onto the earth's crust. I bank the embers of my dying campfire and taste the perfumed juniper smoke that twists and rolls and lays flat over smooth rock terraces. I drift, glad for this life, blessed by the Goddess as she lifts her veil; then come back to myself . . . breathing it all in, breathing it back out again.

• • •

A working poet, painter and author for over twenty years, John Brandi devotes much of his life teaching creative writing in schools, prisons, juvenile delinquent homes and institutes for the handicapped throughout the United States. He is the recipient of several major awards, including an NEA Writing Fellowship, grants from PEN American Center, a Djerassi Foundation Arts Residency and a retrospective exhibit of his paintings at the University of New Mexico. He has lived and raised his children near Santa Fe since 1970.